Blum, Lucille (Hollander)
     A Rorschach workbook, by Lucille Hollander
Blum, Helen H. Davidson [and] Nina D. Field-
stell.   Foreword by Bruno Klopfer.
[2d ed.]   New York, International Universities
Press [c1975]
     iv, 192 p.   illus.
     Bibliography: p. [194]

1. Rorschach test.   I. Title.

A RORSCHACH WORKBOOK

by

Lucille Hollander Blum
Helen H. Davidson
Nina D. Fieldsteel

Foreword by BRUNO KLOPFER

INTERNATIONAL UNIVERSITIES PRESS, INC.

NEW YORK   NEW YORK

Contents

Foreword, by Bruno Klopfer. 1

Preface 3

Why Score the Rorschach Test? 5

CHAPTER I—General Orientation

    A. Fundamental Principles of Scoring 7

    B. Instruction to the Student. 11

CHAPTER II—Description of Scoring Categories

    A. Scoring Categories for Location of Response 13

        Self-Testing Exercises 34

    B. Scoring Categories for Determinants of the Response. . . . 42

        Self-Testing Exercises

                Form Scores. 47

                Movement Scores. 58

                Color Scores. 72

                Shading Scores. 87

    C. Scoring Categories for Content of the Response. 96

        Self-Testing Exercises 103

    D. Scoring Categories for the Frequency of the Response . . .110

    E. Responses Requiring Multiple Determinant Scores. 112

        Self-Testing Exercises 117

CHAPTER III — The Technique of Tabulation

    A. How to List and Sum Scores 125

    B. When to Tally Scores 126

    C. The Determinant Categories — The Psychograph 126

    D. The Location Categories — Table of Percentages 127

    E. Recording of Other Factors 128

CHAPTER IV — The Technique of Administration

    A. General Considerations 131

    B. The Testing Procedure 131

CHAPTER V — Scoring and Developmental Trends 139

APPENDIX 1 – Keys to Self-Testing Exercises 143

APPENDIX 2 – Sample Records with Keys 153

APPENDIX 3 – Comparative Table of Location and Determinant
                 Scores 193

REFERENCES 195

Foreword

What is called "scoring" within the framework of the Rorschach technique has little in common with the assigning of quantitative values in traditional mental measurements. Its purpose is a threefold one:

1. To delineate those aspects of the raw material in Rorschach records which contain interpretatively promising elements.
2. To make such qualitative elements more amenable to quantitative treatment.
3. To facilitate communication among Rorschach specialists.

Historically speaking, such scoring systems often took the flavor of a local dialect spoken by specialists within a geographical area or among the members of a special cult with all the emotional attachments which happen to go along with it. Since the introduction twenty years ago of the "Individual Record Blank," the scoring system used in the present work has become the prevailing Rorschach dialect in most English-speaking countries.

It usually takes the budding Rorschach specialist three to five years of routine work before he becomes sufficiently familiar with Rorschach material so that the scoring becomes more or less automatic. In fact, some experienced workers develop the illusion that scoring a record becomes unimportant, since they assess the important elements and their proportional representation within a record so automatically and extract their interpretative importance so fully by just reading through a record, that they do not feel the need of spelling out the scoring except for research purposes. It is a long and hard way for most students to come to such a seemingly paradisiacal state of Rorschach work, and the way through the dry desert of routine scoring may even produce early impressions (mirages) that scoring is really not important.

Actually, a precise and exacting scoring is, for most students, the indispensable medium for discovering the finer nuances in the material which they need for adequate interpretation, and usually the scoring improves with increasing interpretative understanding and vice versa. All that has been said thus far about scoring should in no way becloud the following fact: Only a relatively small part of what is interpretatively important can ever be included in a scoring system without making it entirely unwieldly and thus limiting its communicative value. For this same reason any scoring system should spartanically limit itself to essential elements and in turn, this makes it even more important that the beginner should not treat it too lightly.

A workbook should lighten the arduous task of the instructor and reduce the frustrating insecurity of the beginner who cannot yet see the forest for the trees. It is a special pleasure for me to send this Workbook on its way, since among its authors are friends and colleagues whose faithful association with our common field of interest is of such long standing.

Bruno Klopfer, Ph.D.

Preface

A Rorschach Workbook was first published in 1954. It has had six printings and has been used widely in formal college courses as well as by individuals who wish to learn the Rorschach method for determining personality structure. Even in these days of increased questions concerning "testing," there is considerable evidence of the professional worker's reliance on the Rorschach method. It is, in fact, the continued wide use of the Rorschach Workbook that has encouraged this new revised edition.

In the present undertaking, we wanted to make the use of the Workbook a more comprehensive learning experience than previously provided for the beginning student. Therefore we have included in the revised edition information on administrative techniques with young children and adolescents as well as with adults. In addition to the two adult records that appear in the earlier edition, we have added three records, one of a young child, one of a child of middle years, and a record of an early adolescent. The student will also find helpful the new section on developmental expectations at various age levels.

The Workbook introduces the student to the procedure for eliciting responses to the cards. It also gives him an understanding of how to translate the raw data thus obtained into letter symbols which constitute the quantitative basis for interpretation. The focus of the Workbook remains the technique of administration and the problems of scoring in preparation for interpretation. The Workbook will serve most effectively as a learning device when used in conjunction with an introductory course in the Rorschach method.

The administration and scoring herein described follow the approach presented by Klopfer and Davidson in their text, The Rorschach Technique and in the text by Klopfer et al., Developments in the Rorschach Technique. Other approaches to scoring are indicated in the comparative table, which is presented in Appendix 3.

The experience gained from the exercises in this Workbook should enable the student to administer and score a Rorschach record with competence. It should also lead to a greater readiness to master the intricacies of interpretation.

We thank Louis Getoff for his assistance with the first edition.

Why Score the Rorschach Test?

The Rorschach test is based upon the assumption that behavior is meaningful. It is also based on the assumption that when a person is presented with unfamiliar, nonstructured material, he will behave in his own individual way. Perception is a significant dimension of human behavior and may be broadly considered to include not only the way a person sees things but also the way he verbalizes the associations that occur to him in connection with his perceptions. It is through this dimension of perception that the Rorschach reveals to us the structure of the personality.

The stimulus material, the ten cards of the Rorschach test, are relatively unstructured. Each card can be seen in many different ways. Each person brings to the test his own personality, his own unique complex of feelings, and his own unique history of experiences. And we find, therefore, that each person structures these ink blots in a way that distinguishes him from the next person.

As we study each person's responses to the cards we become interested in many aspects of his test performance. Working from the assumption that perception is selective we note what our subject selects to perceive. Are the areas selected all encompassing? Are they large? Are they small? Have they been rarely or commonly used by others who have taken the test?

If you look at the ten blots you will note that they possess certain qualities. Some have color while others do not; the colors vary in hue and intensity. Some areas of the blots are heavily shaded and others are not. Some blots appear very black and others less so. And each blot has a different shape. How then does each subject respond to these qualities? Does he respond to the shape only? Does he use or avoid the colored areas? Does he select the colored areas for his response but without using the color values? And if he does use the colors in his response, how does he use them? Do the colors fit the response? Is the response based solely on the color? The same questions concerning the subject's handling of the shading properties of the cards might be asked.

Some persons imbue their percepts with life. The people they see seem to be alive, their animals may appear to be in action, they may project movement into inanimate objects. Which of these does your subject do?

We wish also to know which of all the things we have discussed our subject does not do; i.e., we are concerned not only with what he selects to perceive but also with what he selects not to perceive.

There are other things we must also note: the clarity or quality of

each response, the order in which they are given, the speed of responding, the subject's certainty or uncertainty about his responses,
and so forth.

As you go on to study the interpretation of the Rorschach test you
will explore the possible meanings of these different ways of responding to the blots and their implications for the personality you are
studying.

In order to attempt to interpret each person's total reaction to the
test, it is first necessary to describe each response in terms of the
area selected, the quality of the blot used, the frequency of the response, and the like, and then examine the existing relationships
among the responses. An aid in this understanding of the individual's
response to the test is the use of a symbolic shorthand which can be
easily manipulated. If we can capture the gist of each perception, of
each response in a symbol, we can then examine our subject's performance in quantifiable terms. (Note that although a quantitative
analysis of the responses in terms of scores is invaluable for the
interpretative summary of a Rorschach protocol, the actual responses
are always used to estimate qualitative aspects of the performance
without which a Rorschach interpretation lacks validity.) We can then
readily determine how frequently the subject uses a particular area
of the blot, how often he responds to a particular quality of the blot,
and the extent to which he varies what he sees. More important, the
descriptive symbols will permit us to compare our subject's perceptions and evaluate them in the light of the perceptions which we expect
from defined groups of people. Scoring thus becomes a frame of
reference for the interpretation of a Rorschach protocol.

Chapter I
General Orientation

A. Fundamental Principles of Scoring

1. Function of Scoring

   The scoring categories have been developed to enable the worker to convert the formal aspects of the responses into symbols which are needed for the interpretation of the record. The scoring category must serve the following functions:

   (1) It should indicate the relation between the subject's response and the elements in the blot material which were used in the formation of the concept.
   (2) It should be so defined as to make a specific contribution with respect to the interpretive procedure.

2. What Is a Response?

   A response is a separate idea or concept which is given in relation to a specific aspect or area of the blot material. Responses are divided into two categories: main and additional.

   Main responses are independent concepts given at the time the cards are initially presented to the subject. This phase of administration is called the "performance proper."

   Additional responses are independent concepts given when the cards are presented for the second time. This phase of administration is called the "inquiry."

3. What Is Scored?

   Each response is scored for location, determinant, content, and whether popular or original. These scores may be main scores or additional scores. The accuracy of the concept in terms of fit to the blot area selected may also be scored and is referred to as form-level rating.[1]

   The main scores are those given to the essential aspect of a response elicited during the performance proper. A response may have only one main location score, only one main determinant score, one main content score and one main original-popular score, if the latter is required.

[1] Form-level rating as a fifth dimension of scoring is now used by Klopfer et al. (1954) and fully described in Chapter 8 of their text This aspect of scoring is not employed in the Workbook.

Additional scores may occur under the following different circumstances.

(1) Scores needed beyond the main score to describe completely a response given during the performance proper.
(2) Elaborations or new associations elicited during the inquiry to responses already given during the performance proper.
(3) New responses given during the inquiry.
(4) Main responses which are rejected during the inquiry.

There may be any number of additional scores needed to describe a concept, although there is usually not more than two additional scores needed.

Each response is also considered in terms of quality; that is, does the shape of the blot area selected conform to the acceptable shape of the concept seen? The quality levels are: adequate, markedly superior form and poor form.

Location scores indicate which part and how much of the blot area the concept involves. These areas may be the whole blot or a usual or unusual part of the blot. Whether the subject uses the whole blot or part of the blot for his response provides useful information for the understanding of his personality.

Determinant scores indicate which of the various qualities of the blot material the subject used and which he might have projected in the formation of a concept. These qualities are form, movement, color and shading.

(1) Form scores refer to responses which use only the outline or contour of the blot.
(2) Movement scores refer to responses where there is a kinesthetic projection onto the blot material.
(3) Color scores refer to responses which make use of the chromatic or achromatic properties of the blot.
(4) Shading scores refer to responses which make use of light-dark properties of the blot either for surface, texture, or for depth or diffusion.

An analysis of how often and in what way the subject uses and projects these qualities is essential in describing his personality characteristics.

4. Use of Symbols in Scoring

a. Major Scoring Symbols

The scoring symbols used to score location, determinant, content, and whether the concept is popular or original, are, in most instances, the first letter of the word from which it is derived. Scoring symbols are capital letters, small letters, and letter combinations. The scoring symbols used in this Workbook are presented below with a brief explanation of each.

Location Scores

W	Whole response (all or nearly all of blot used)
Ŵ	Incomplete whole (at least 2/3 of blot)
DW	Confabulatory whole
D	Large usual detail
d	Small usual detail
Dd^2	Unusual detail
dd	Tiny detail
de	Edge detail
di	Inner detail
dr	Rare detail
S	White space

Determinant Scores

Form Scores

F	Adequate form
F−	Poor form
F+	Markedly superior form

Movement Scores

M	Human movement
FM	Animal movement
Fm, mF	Inanimate movement in combination with form
m	Inanimate movement without form

Color Scores

FC, CF	Chromatic color in combination with form
C	Chromatic color without form
F/C, C/F	Arbitrary combination of chromatic color with form
FC', C'F	Achromatic color in combination with form
C'	Achromatic color without form

---

^{2}Dd is not a scoring symbol but is used to designate the classification, Unusual Detail. The four symbols under the Dd classification are those used in the actual scoring.

Shading Scores

Fc, cF Surface texture or appearance in combination with form

c   Surface and texture response without form

FK   Vista

KF   Diffusion in combination with form

K   Diffusion without form

Fk, kF Representative distance response in combination with form

k   Representative distance without form

Content Scores

H	Human figures
Hd	Parts of human figures
A	Animal figures
Ad	Parts of living animals
AObj	Fur skins, skulls, etc.
At	Human anatomy
Obj	Man-made objects
N	Nature
Geo	Topographical and outline maps and geographical concepts
Sex	

Popular — Original Scores

P	Popular response
O	Original response

b. Minor Scoring Symbols

In addition to the scoring symbols presented above, minor symbols are sometimes needed to describe more specifically how the concept was formed. These minor scoring symbols are commas (,) used to indicate that the subject actually employs more than one location area or determinant or content in his response, arrows (⟶) to indicate that the subject's response tends to employ another location area, or another determinant, or another content as an elaboration to his main concept, and brackets (}) used to indicate that the subject tends to combine two or more concepts into a single idea. All letter scores placed after the minor scoring symbols are additional scores.

B. Instruction to the Student

The scoring categories for location of the response (where the concept was seen), the determinant of the response (how the concept was seen), the content of the response (what was seen), the originality or popularity of the response (how frequently a concept is perceived) are defined and illustrated in Chapter II. Sample items to illustrate the specific categories are presented. Self-testing exercises are given after each of the six major sections. Further exercises in scoring are given in Chapter II, Section E to aid the student in learning multiple determinant scoring.

Keys to all the scoring exercises including the sample records are given in Appendix 1. The complete scoring, that is, for location, determinant, content, and whether popular or original, is given for each exercise item. The symbol that is underlined is the one which pertains to the scoring category under consideration.

The responses have been taken from actual Rorschach records. Throughout the Workbook the response given during the "performance proper" is indicated first. Additional information obtained during "the inquiry" is separated from the "performance" response by a space.

Chapter II

Description of Scoring Categories

The Rorschach scoring categories have been developed to describe the subject's productions in terms of four structural qualities of the blot material:

Where on the card was the concept seen (Location)
How was the concept seen (Determinant)
What was seen (Content)
How commonly is the concept seen by other persons
    (Popular — Original)

A. Scoring Categories for Location of Response

1. General Meaning and Definition of the Location Score

    Location refers to what part of the blot material was used in the formation of the concept. Location responses may be differentiated into whole or virtually whole responses and detail responses.

2. Definition and Samples of the Whole Score

    The whole response implies the use of the entire blot area or the intention to use the whole blot area for the formation of a concept. There are several ways in which the whole blot can be used. Different scoring symbols indicate these variations: W W̊ DW

    a. Whole (W) implies the use of the entire blot material excluding the white space for the formation of the concept.

Card I[1]	∨ Looks like a bat or something.
Card II	Could resemble two bears, the heads are here (upper red), and their legs are bleeding (lower red).
Card III	Looks like two men bowling, facing each other, just about to throw the ball, down at end where pins are (center red), and there (upper red) are lights hanging from the ceiling.

[1] These symbols, ∧∨><, are used to indicate the position in which the subject holds the card as he gives his response. The apex always represents the top of the card.

Card VII   ∨ Two girls dancing with cloud over-
head.

b. Incomplete whole. (W)signifies the use of at least two
thirds of the blot in the formation of the particular
concept. The subject must have intentionally omitted
parts of the blot which do not fit the concept.

Card I   (whole card except wing projections) A
cat's face here without those parts
sticking out on the side.

Card II   (whole blot except upper and lower red)
Two bears dancing with each other.

Card V   A bat, but these (side extensions) do
not belong.

Card VI   This looks like a bear rug except for
this top part.

c. Confabulatory whole (DW) is used for responses where
a small portion of the blot is clearly perceived and
the whole is then forced into an interpretation suggested by the original percept. A DW response is always by definition a poor form response.

Card IV   It's a lobster because this part (side
extension) looks like the claw of a
lobster.

Card VI   A cat because these look like cat's
whiskers and the rest is the body.

Card II   A butterfly, all of it, because these
(lower red extensions) look like feelers.

Card IX   Can't seem to see anything, feelers up
here (upper center D) Oh, it all must
be an insect.

3. Definition and Samples of the Detail Score

The detail response implies the use of part of the blot in
the formation of a concept. Detail responses are differentiated on the basis of whether the area is an obvious, easily
delineated and frequently selected portion of the blot or is
an unusual area and less frequently used. The obvious, frequently used areas are called the usual details and are
scored: D or d depending on the size of the area. The less
obvious and less frequently used areas are called the unusual details and are scored with the symbols dd, de, di, dr.

a. The Usual Large and Small Detail (D and d)
The D and d symbols imply the use of portions of the
blot which are clearly set off and are the most frequently used areas for the formation of a concept.

D refers to relatively large portions of the blot; d to smaller portions of the blot. The areas represented by D and d are limited in number and specifically delineated. Following is a list of the usual details (D and d) for each card with an identifying response to each area.[2]
D and d areas are delineated in the blots which follow. The number on the blot refers to the number in the list which describes that part of the location area.

LARGE (D) AND SMALL (d) USUAL DETAIL RESPONSES TO CARDS I-X, IN APPROXIMATE ORDER OF FREQUENCY

Card I

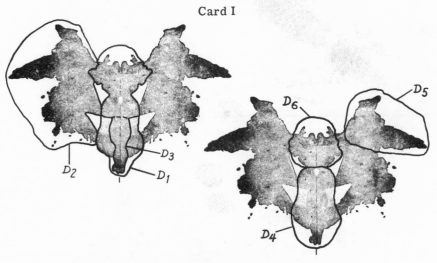

Large Usual Detail (D)

1. Entire center ("woman's body") with or without lighter gray (transparent skirt) in lower portion
2. Entire side (witch, bear)
3. Lower center without lighter gray (thighs and legs)
4. Entire lower center (bell)
5. Upper side (dog's head with snout outside)
6. Upper third of center (crab)

---

[2] The list of usual details (D and d) is taken from Klopfer and Davidson (1962, pp. 52-63). The student should be aware that some latitude must be allowed in the delineation of these areas.

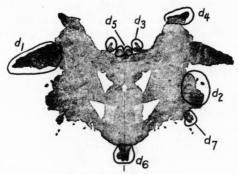

Small Usual Detail (d)

1. Upper outer projections (wings)
2. Lower side (lady's head)
3. Upper, inner, claw-like extensions (hands)
4. Uppermost projections (bear's head)
5. Upper innermost details (heads)
6. Bottom projection (feet)
7. Small knob-like extension at lower side (sheaf of wheat)

Card II

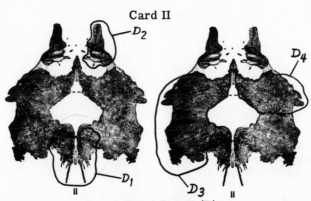

Large Usual Detail (D)

1. Lower red with or without black-red mixture (butterfly)
2. Upper red (Christmas stockings)
3. Entire side black (bear, dog)
4. Upper portion of black (one half to one third)

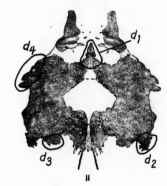

Small Usual Detail (d)

1. Upper center (castle)
2. Bottom outer projection (hen's head)
3. Bottom projection adjacent to preceding d (Indian head)
4. Upper side projection (stone head)

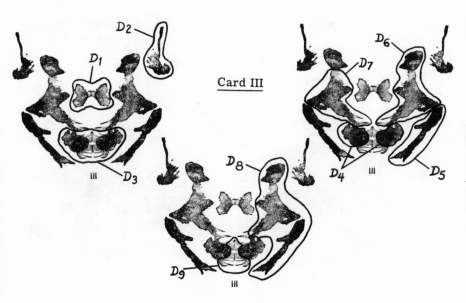

Card III

Large Usual Detail (D)

1. Inner red (butterfly or bow)
2. Outer red with or without tail-like extension
3. Entire lower center (pelvis or mask)
4. Lower center black (Negro heads)
5. Lower side black (fish or hand)
6. Upper side black—head and upper part of body of the usual figure (bird on rock, card inverted)
7. Middle side black (airplane)
8. One of the two human figures
9. Lower center light gray (ribs)

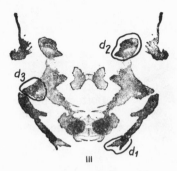

Small Usual Detail (d)

1. Bottom side portion (high-heeled shoes) with or without lower part of "leg"
2. Top side black (head)
3. Side black lateral protrusion usually upside down as animal head (with tiny white space as eye)

Card IV

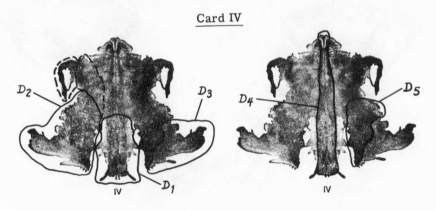

Large Usual Detail (D)

1. Lower center (animal head)
2. Lower side black and gray sometimes including the upper side portion (boot)
3. Lower side light gray (dog)
4. Entire vertical dark center
5. Inner dark side detail (nuns, card inverted)

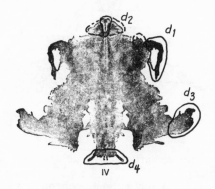

Small Usual Detail (d)

1. Upper side extension (snake) sometimes with small adjacent portion (dancer with face in adjoining portion)
2. Uppermost portion (flower) sometimes including adjacent shade portion (Japanese face)
3. Outermost lower side extension (head of dog)
4. Lowermost portion of lower center detail (crown)

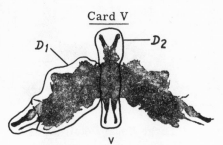

Large Usual Detail (D)

1. Entire side with or without light gray extensions (face or figure lying down)
2. Center vertical portion (rabbit)

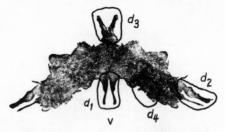

Small Usual Detail (d)

1. Bottom (tweezers)
2. Side extension (leg) sometimes with adjacent thin extension
   , (crocodile's head)
3. Top (rabbit's head), or top without uppermost protrusions, (police-
   man's head)
4. Contour of lower side detail (profile)

Card VI

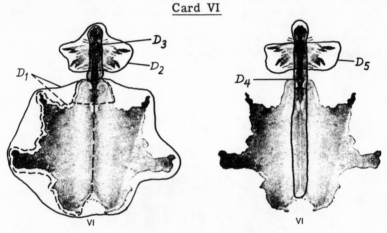

Large Usual Detail (D)

1. Entire lower portion (animal skin) or half of lower portion (boat or
   king's head)
2. Entire upper portion (dragonfly) sometimes including light gray
   uppermost portion of lower detail (lighthouse on rock with beacon)
3. Upper black portion only of center column (snake) sometimes without slightly shaded outer portion
4. Entire dark vertical center (spine)
5. Lighter part only of upper portion (wings)

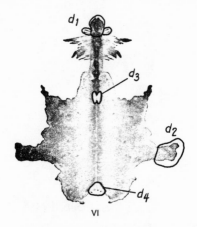

Small Usual Detail (d)

1. Uppermost detail (snake's head) with or without "whiskers"
2. Lower lateral extensions (dog's head)
3. Two inner light gray ovals (mice)
4. Bottom inner projections (birds or eggs in nest)

Card VII

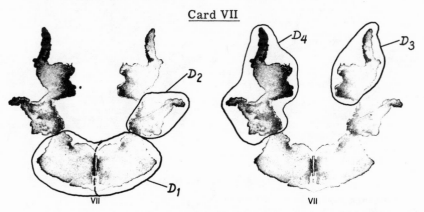

Large Usual Detail (D)

1. Entire bottom portion (butterfly) sometimes each half separate (sheep)
2. Middle third (mask)
3. Upper third, with or without uppermost projection (woman's head)
4. Upper two thirds (dog)

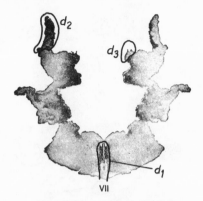

Small Usual Detail (d)

1. Dark center bottom detail (canal)
2. Top projections (squirrel's tail)
3. Light gray projections on upper inner corner of top third (icicles)

Card VIII

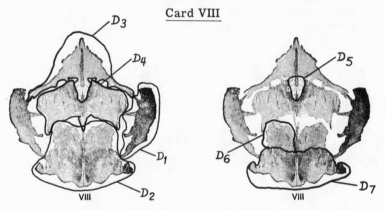

Large Usual Detail (D)

1. Side pink (animals)
2. Lower pink and orange (butterfly)
3. Top gray portion with or without center line (mountain and tree)
   sometimes including rib-like figure and/or blue portion
4. Middle blue portion (flags)
5. Rib-like figure in upper center (spine)
6. Bottom pink alone (bullfrog heads)
7. Bottom orange alone

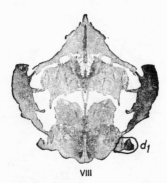

VIII

Small Usual Detail (d)

1. Lateral extensions of bottom orange (lamb's head)

Card IX

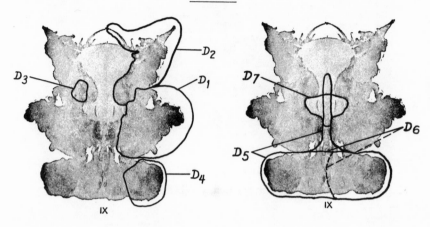

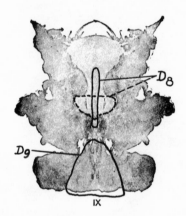

Large Usual Detail (D)

1. Green portion
2. Orange portion
3. Small inner portion at junction of green and orange (deer's head)
4. Lateral pink (man's head)
5. Entire pink portion plus center line (tree), card inverted
6. Entire pink or either half
7. Center portion between lateral greens (skull)
8. Center gray portion (candle), with or without preceding D
9. Inner pink portion (elephants' heads)

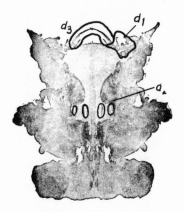

Small Usual Detail (d)

1. All or most of upper inner orange projections (lobster claws)
2. Eye-like portion in middle including green and white slits (eyes)
3. Arch-like light orange at top center

Card X

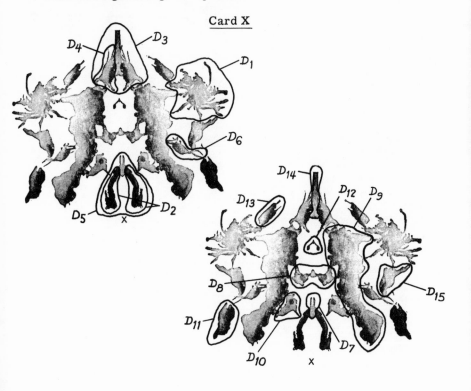

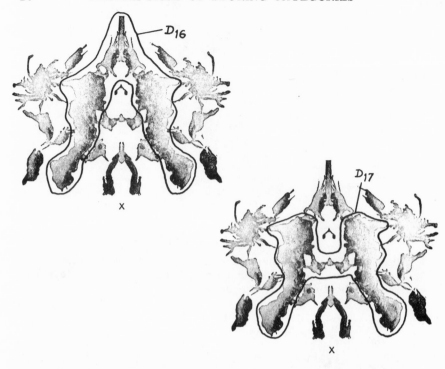

1. Outer blue (crabs) sometimes with outer green
2. Inner green, dark portions only (caterpillars)
3. Entire gray portion at top
4. Gray "animals" at top, without inner gray column
5. Entire inner green
6. Outer gray-brown figures (mice)
7. Light portion between inner greens (rabbit's head)
8. Inner blue (birds)
9. Pink portion separately (mountain)
10. Inner yellow (lions or dogs)
11. Outer orange (collie dog)
12. Inner orange (wishbone)
13. Outer upper green (grasshopper)
14. Gray column at top without gray "animals" beside it
15. Outer yellow
16. Pink with entire top gray (flowers), card inverted
17. Pink with inner blue (man on a mountain or cliff)

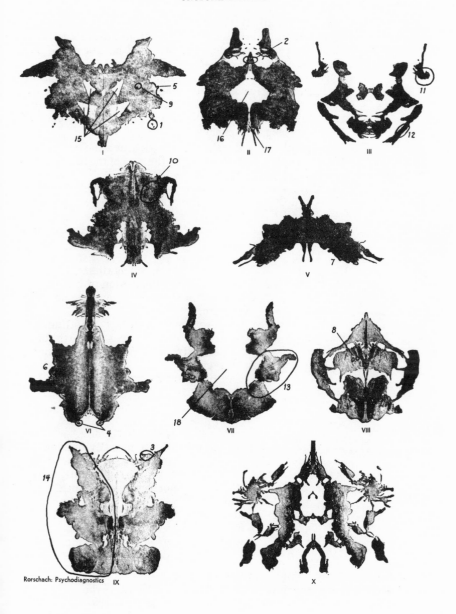

b. The Unusual Detail (Dd)

Dd (unusual detail) signifies use of a portion of the blot which is not a usual large or small detail area, not a whole or space area. Dd responses vary with respect to the size of the area used, placement on the blot or how clearly it stands out from the blot or other uncommon delineation of an area generally seen in another way.

To differentiate these possibilities, the Dd symbol is subdivided into four scores which are the ones actually used in the scoring of such responses:

(1) [3]Tiny detail (dd) refers to responses which use tiny areas which are easily delineated from the rest of the blot material.

  1. Card I   Question mark.
  2. Card II   Like a black bow-tie.
  3. Card IX   A map of Italy.
  4. Card VI   Two monkeys.

(2) Edge detail (de) signifies the use of only the contour or outline of the edge of the blot.

  5. Card I   Mountain.
                 Just the profile of mountains.
  6. Card VI   Edge gives the impression of a face.
                 Outline of profile, nose, mouth open, chin.
  7. Card V   Coastline.
                 Edge down here looks like coastline.

(3) Inner detail (di) signifies the use of an area inside the blot which is not easily delineated from the rest of the blot material.

  8. Card VIII   Bird's-eyes.
                 Looks like a bird's small eyes.
  9. Card I   Coin.
                 Ancient coin, not quite round edges.
  10. Card IV   Woman's face.
                 Here's nose, eye, flowing hair.

(4) Rare detail (dr) refers to the use of unusually delineated areas which may be small or large in size, where the area is not scorable as dd, de, di , and where it is sufficiently different from a D, d or W̄ that it cannot be scored as such.

  11. Card III   A hen.
  12. Card III   Like a piece of burned wood.
  13. Card VII   A dog sniffing on a pile of refuse.
  14. Card IX   A witch with a green skirt taking off
                 from a red carpet.

4. Definition and Samples of the Space Score

White space score (S) represents concepts using the white area which is either inside the blot or surrounding it. Mere

---

[3]Consult Unusual Details Picture Sheet for the location of the following sample responses numbered 1 to 18.

inclusion of a white area in a concept is not scored.

15. <u>Card I</u>   These four look like triangles.
16. <u>Card II</u>   A ballet dancer on tiptoes.
17. <u>Card II</u>   Chandelier crystals.
18. <u>Card VII</u> George Washington—face and tricorn hat.

5. <u>Combinations of Location Scores</u>[4]

a. <u>Whole Space (W,S)</u> implies the use of the whole blot in combination with a white space where the latter is supplementary in the concept.

<u>Card VII</u>   Looks like some land with water surrounding it and here is a bay.

<u>Card VIII</u> Like the inside of your body with the ribs showing, all these are different organs.

<u>Card I</u>   Looks like a mask, here are the eyes, mouth, and two ears.

<u>Card II</u>   A volcano and this part is the crater, these are the flames (D2).

b. <u>Detail Space (D,S)</u> refers to use of a large usual detail combined with a white space.

<u>Card II</u>   A fancy lampshade (D1) with a white globe attached to it.

<u>Card I</u>   This part (D1) looks like a cat from Alice in Wonderland with big eyes, mouth. Looks awful.

<u>Card VIII</u> Here are ribs (D5) and these are the spaces in between.

c. <u>Detail Tendency to Whole (D—→W)</u> is used in those instances where a large detail is clearly perceived and then the subject attempts to integrate the rest of the blot material in an indefinite way or the subject during the inquiry enlarges his percept to include the rest of the blot.

<u>Card I</u>   Two Santa Clauses (D2) carrying Christmas trees. The rest looks like a stage setting.

<u>Card VII</u>   This looks like smoke here (D1). Now I see it's rising and as it rises, it turns into two little boys.

<u>Card VIII</u> Two animals (D1) walking over some beautiful rocks and in the middle, there is water.

d. <u>Details Combined Into Whole</u> $\left(\begin{smallmatrix}D\\D\end{smallmatrix}\right\}W\right)$ implies the use of two or more large usual details for the formation of separate concepts which relate to one another and are then drawn into a concept which involves the total blot.

---

[4]Location scores may be combined in many different ways. The more common combinations, with samples, are presented here.

<u>Card IX</u>   Two witches (D2) dancing around a cauldron — there is fire and smoke (D1 and D6).

<u>Card III</u>   This reminds me of birds (D8). Here is one sitting in a nest (D3) and these (D2) are flying.

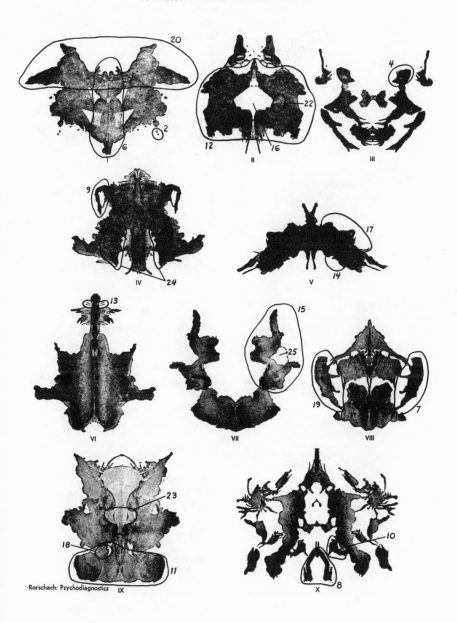

Rorschach: Psychodiagnostics

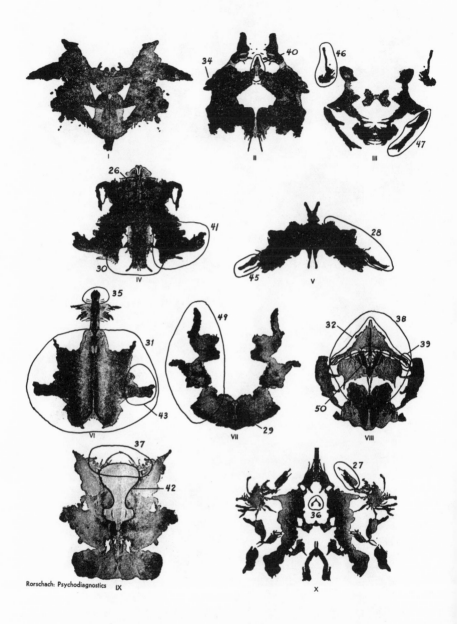

Rorschach: Psychodiagnostics

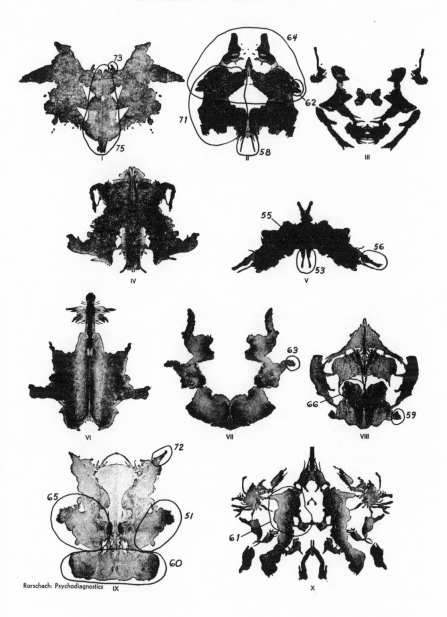

Rorschach: Psychodiagnostics

SELF-TESTING EXERCISES—LOCATION SCORES

Ex.[5] No.	Card No.		Loc.	Det.	Con.	P-Q

Consult Location Scores Picture Sheet A

1	V	A bat.				
		Wings outstretched, ears, can't tell which side is facing, a diagrammatic representation.	___	___	___	___
2	I	Particles of dust.	___	___	___	___
3	VI	A hide spread out.				
		A hide, jagged pointed edges, tail on pole, rest hanging down spread out.	___	___	___	___
4	III	Head of a bird.				
		Could be an ant eater head because of the snout.	___	___	___	___
5	VIII	Alice in Wonderland animals climbing rocks.				
		Climbing up rocks.	___	___	___	___
6	I	Middle looks like a figure without a head, with a belt.				
		Collar, belt and belt buckle like a doll or figurine. The man could have wings; more of a man than a woman, sort of a superman with wings.	___	___	___	___
7	VIII	A mole.				
		A mole in climbing position but not moving.	___	___	___	___
8	X	Glow worms.				
		Just plain worms.	___	___	___	___

[5]Exercise numbers 1-25 are on Picture Sheet for Location Scores A; numbers 26-50 on Picture Sheet for Location Scores B; 51-75 on Picture Sheet for Location Scores C. All the exercises are shown in this way.

Ex. No.	Card No.		Loc.	Det.	Con.	P-O
9	IV	A woman diving.				
		A jackknife dive into the sea.	___	___	___	___
10	X	Dancers stretched out on floor in costume.				
		Dancers resting on arm stretched out on floor.	___	___	___	___
11	IX	∨Something or something's shoulders holding something up.				
		Here are the hands, something could be crouching with the hands holding up the end.	___	___	___	___
12	II	Stage curtains being pulled apart, center shows lighted stage.				
		Stage curtains would bunch this way. Stage is white from bright lights.	___	___	___	___
13	VI	Cat's whiskers but no cat, just whiskers.	___	___	___	___
14	V	Face of a woman.				
		Head of woman, hand over forehead contrasts to white of forehead.	___	___	___	___
15	VII	Child sticking its tongue out.				
		Upturned nose, looks impish.	___	___	___	___
16	II	Skate in middle, ocean fish.				
		Shape, tail coming out.	___	___	___	___
17	V	Craggy mountain area.				
		Craggy dark wood area, irregular formation bare as you see in mountains sometimes.	___	___	___	___
18	IX	Chinese hands with long fingers coming down.	___	___	___	___

Ex. No.	Card No.		Loc.	Det.	Con.	P-O
19	VIII	Could be two tigers climbing up on mountain. All rest part of mountains.	___	___	___	___
20	I	Birds perched out, up.				
		Birds perched, wings up.	___	___	___	___
21	III	Two men in full dress in conflict over organs of woman which are swinging, hanging, hitting men in head. The men are overcivilized, birdlike, too refined, too effeminate. Bow tie in middle symbolic of party-color.				
		An unreal carnival-like Hallowe'en party; shoes like cloven hoofs, bodies bent. Conflict over pelvis fundamental.	___	___	___	___
22	II	Blurred man.				
		Saw eye, nose and moustache.	___	___	___	___
23	IX	Animal figure.				
		Eyes, ears, nostrils, looks like animal, incomplete head.	___	___	___	___
24	IV ∨	Two witches in dark part.				
		Caps, noses, scrawny incomplete figures, standing there.	___	___	___	___
25	VII ∨	A dog's face.				
		Like a collie.	___	___	___	___

Consult Location Scores Picture Sheet B

26	IV ∨	Dog face with one eye sticking out, something like my dog — this one looks angry.				
		Only eyes frightened, distrustful like wild eyes.	___	___	___	___
27	X	Little dog, whole body — like when held up in arms and it's kicking.	___	___	___	___

Ex. No.	Card No.		Loc.	Det.	Con.	P-O
28	V	Female figure resting. Not too clear.				
		Arm bent, body reclining, female leg.	—	—	—	—
29	VII	Female organ.				
		Center organ, line of opening, dark area around, black hair around the opening.	—	—	—	—
30	IV	∨ Imperial German — Eagle type.				
		Too vague to me so I can't describe it.	—	—	—	—
31	VI	A piece of moldy bread.				
		Shading-mold forming on bread mass.	—	—	—	—
32	VIII	Animal figure made of white, hooded effect almost to eyes.				
		Eyes, snout, fur, irregular shape white fur, hooded effect.	—	—	—	—
33	I	Mask — cat face.				
		Grinning cat face mask, eyes, ears, mouth.	—	—	—	—
34	II	Indian profile, outline of nose and strong jaw.	—	—	—	—
35	VI	Cat-like head with whiskers. Cat head and whiskers.	—	—	—	—
36	X	Wishbone.				
		Shape.	—	—	—	—
37	IX	Clothes line with clothes hanging on it.	—	—	—	—

Ex. No.	Card No.		Loc.	Det.	Con.	P-O
38	VIII	A Viking ship with headmast.				
		Here's the headmast, is that what they call it? About half of the ship is here.	___	___	___	___
39	VIII	Lobster claw.				
		Coming up out of the water, things seem to be dragged up with it.	___	___	___	___
40	II	Vise holds tools, holds things together.				
		Sections of vise that grasps things.	___	___	___	___
41	IV	Foot upraised.				
		Almost a dance movement.	___	___	___	___
42	IX	An hourglass.				
		Not a good one, distorts time because not the same size on top and on bottom.	___	___	___	___
43	VI	Head, eyes, long forehead, nose, jowls, beard.				
		Nose, eyes, and beard of a man.	___	___	___	___
44	VII	Heads and busts, hands outstretched in movement.				
		Looks like girls playing with one another with hands out over here. Not this part [D1].	___	___	___	___
45	V	Couple of horses with elongated faces scooting out of thing, look like Picasso horses.				
		Jaw out, foreleg coming out, rushing out at great speed, almost horizontal.	___	___	___	___
46	III	A bagpipe.				
		Tube, wind bag, shape.	___	___	___	___

Ex. No.	Card No.		Loc.	Det.	Con.	P-O
47	III	Map of Italy.				
		General shape of Italy.	——	——	——	——
48	V	Flying rabbit with two overbig wings.				
		Rabbit with ears, wings, attitude of flying.	——	——	——	——
49	VII	Scotties.				
		I don't know why I see scotties, I don't like them. One seems to be attached to the head of another. Maybe they're toys that are stuck and one is broken off at the head.	——	——	——	——
50	VIII	Back of skull.				
		Back of skull, open areas.	——	——	——	——

Consult Location Scores Picture Sheet C

Ex. No.	Card No.		Loc.	Det.	Con.	P-O
51	IX	Looks like a little pig.				
		A pig romping. Square part here the nose.	——	——	——	——
52	I	Could be a tree branch with a pair of falcons or birds on it.				
		The branch in middle — the way it's shaped, the knots in it, and the way the supposed bird is. Looks like ready to go after something. Could be a pair of hunting birds.	——	——	——	——
53	V ∨	Snakes ready to come up. Indian snake charmer's.				
		Snakes head up, ready to come up.	——	——	——	——
54	I	Horrible bug flying around.				
		Grasping mouth and jaws, wings out, attacking, predatory.	——	——	——	——

Ex. No.	Card No.		Loc.	Det.	Con.	P-O
55	V	See a couple of eyes in middle of things, eyes of insect in wrong spot.				
		Might be. Some bugs have eyes all over, caterpillars have two rows of eyes, these eyes are like that.	—	—	—	—
56	V	A leg — could be an animal walking toward you.				
		Here is the leg, the rest is some sort of animal.	—	—	—	—
57	II	Patty cake, patty cake, baker's man. It's really two pinheads in a circus playing pattycake.				
		Heads strange shaped, not really pinheads but makes me think of people who put rings on children's heads when young and put a smaller one on each year 'til it's shaped like this. They'd belong only in a circus.	—	—	—	—
58	II	Antennae of insect.				
		Forward portion of insect doesn't fit into any standard category. Rather strange.	—	—	—	—
59	VIII	An animal head, some kind of terrier.	—	—	—	—
60	IX	I think my guts look like that.				
		Part of intestine's humpy outline here like you see in drawings. I suppose it's the color, it all looks like intestines opened up.	—	—	—	—
61	X	Things playing on little bagpipes.				
		Dribbles out into sort of ectoplasm, like babies' round shape and pug noses, blowing bagpipes.	—	—	—	—

Ex. No.	Card No.		Loc.	Det.	Con.	P-O
62	II	Back of rabbit's ears.				
		Two ears back of rabbit's head.	___	___	___	___
63	VII	Colon.				
		Looks like a picture of a colon.	___	___	___	___
64	II	Two ladies in turbans playing cards.				
		They look like they are not trying very hard to hide their hands. Don't know what this is.	___	___	___	___
65	IX	< Old woman bent over scrubbing. Apron tied up behind her.	___	___	___	___
66	VIII	Head of stone, looks like a stone monument.				
		Head here - a monument.	___	___	___	___
67	III	Two men with beards, white celluloid collars and dress suits.				
		Caricature of men bowing to center figure. And this part does not belong [D2].	___	___	___	___
68	III	Looks like a funny-book page.				
		Looks like the Gumps, talking maybe, but like something added for a little color.	___	___	___	___
69	IX	This way like fruit — 4 beets, 2 cabbages, 2 carrots.				
		Beets, red; cabbages, green; carrots, orange.	___	___	___	___
70	IV	A man sitting on a tree stump.	___	___	___	___
71	II	Head of a teddy bear.				
		Head of a soft stuffed animal, ears floppy.	___	___	___	___

Ex. No.	Card No.		Loc.	Det.	Con.	P-O
72	IX	Carrot.				
		Color and shape	___	___	___	___
73	I	Happy little clowns looking at each other.				
		Bald, grotesque, gleeful clowns. Little tall hats, faces sticking out playfully.	___	___	___	___
74	IX	White thing started out distinctly, leaves fallen on whole pattern.				
		Started out as distinct whitish background, leaves on it now. Shapes of fallen leaves.	___	___	___	___
75	I	Woman's figure without a head.				
		Belted with bustles, busts, a manikin.	___	___	___	___

B. Scoring Categories for Determinants of the Response

   1. General Meaning and Definition of the Determinant Score

Determinant scores indicate how the subject uses the perceptual qualities of the blot. The use of one of these qualities (form, movement, color, or shading) or a combination of two or more is described by the determinant scores. Since more than one determinant is often needed to describe a response, an order of preference for determinant scores is suggested when the subject's response does not indicate clearly which determinant is "main" and which is "additional." The order of preference recommended is: human movement scores take precedence, then animal movement, followed by color and then shading.

    a. Form Level or Quality of the Response

The quality of the form involved in all responses is an important consideration in evaluating the function of the personality. Responses have either vague forms like "clouds" or "smoke," or definite forms like "red bow tie," "bear's head" or "two men bowing." Where the vague form response is appropriate to the blot area (ex. "Clouds" — Card VII) it is not scored either plus or minus. Responses with definite forms should be evaluated as to the accuracy of the perceived form; that is, does the outline of the blot area used bear a resemblance to the given concept. Responses which are inadequate in form are scored minus. Responses which are markedly superior in accuracy are scored plus. Mediocre form accuracy is indicated by the determinant symbol alone, without either the qualifying plus or minus.[6]

2. Definition and Samples of the Form Score
     Form scores indicate the use of only the outline or shape or contour of the blot to determine the concept. These responses are scored F. The accuracy of the form may be designated in two ways: Plus and minus, or by a numerical value.[6]

    a. Form (F) implies responses determined by shape alone where the shape is adequate.

Card I	An emblem or a coat of arms (W)
Card V	Tweezers—that a lady might use (dl)
Card III	This red part in the middle looks like a butterfly (D1). (Q) Oh no, there are no red butterflies; it's just the shape.
Card VII	Smoke (W)

    b. Superior Form (F+) indicates the use of an area, the shape of which is especially well delineated.

Card V	Profile of a man, old-fashioned haircut, strong nose, moustache upturned, and long beard; Victorian appearance (D1)
Card X	Show poodle, hair cut to look like wide collar and narrow body (D10).
Card IV	An old shoe, heel coming off, toes turned up, outline shows wrinkled leather (D2).

    c. Poor Form (F–) indicates the use of an area, the shape of which clearly deviates from the realistic shape of the concept offered.

Card V	Kangaroo—the legs look like kangaroo's (d1).
Card II	A coat. There's where you open it and here are the sides (Q) just a plain coat (W).
Card II	The whole thing looks like a building with two towers. This part is part of it, but I don't know what (W).

---

[6]The numerical values for form level range from −2.0 to +5.0 and are also applied to other determinant scores. For further description see Klopfer & Davidson, 1962, pp. 95-119.

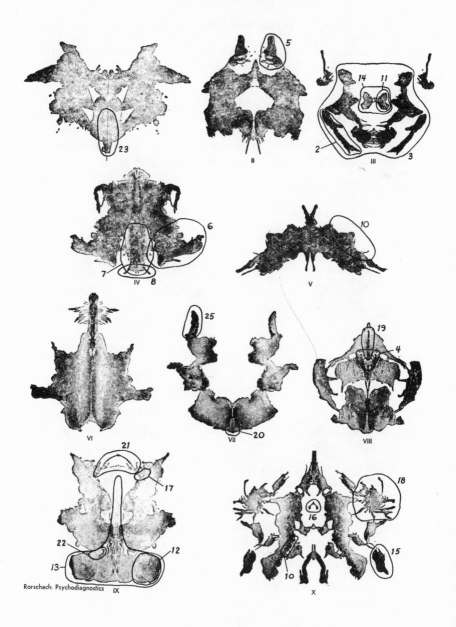

Rorschach: Psychodiagnostics

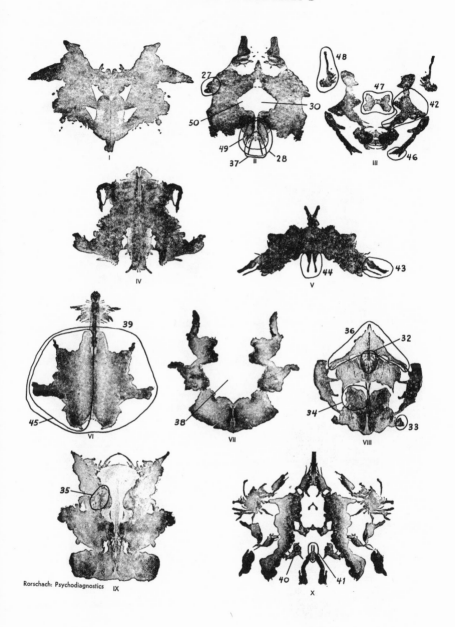

Rorschach: Psychodiagnostics

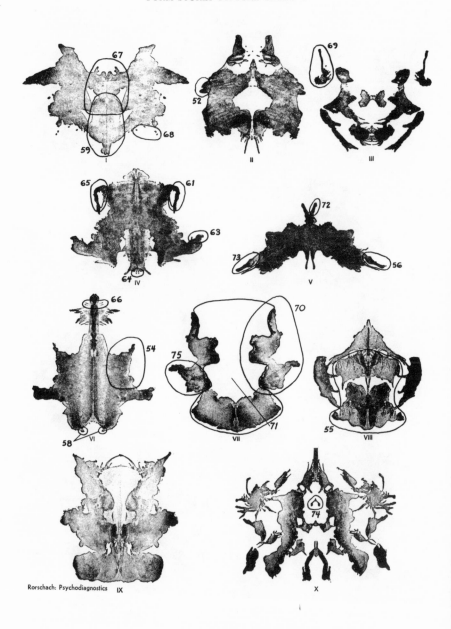

Rorschach: Psychodiagnostics

Ex. No.	Card No.		Loc.	Det.	Con.	P-O

Consult Form Scores Picture Sheet A

1	V	Could be old flying animal that lived in prehistoric times, like a bird, bat. That's all [whole].	——	——	——	——
2	III	Fishes.				
		A long one.	——	——	——	——
3	III	∨ A person.				
		Head, face, one person, body here, bow tie, eyes, mouth.	——	——	——	——
4	VIII	Almost looks like a centipede, projecting legs.				
		Perhaps looks more like a water bug.	——	——	——	——
5	II	Church.				
		This could be the steeple, here the door, I don't know why, it looks like a church to me.	——	——	——	——
6	IV	Looks like sort of shoes of some sort.				
		Boots or overshoes, just the shape.	——	——	——	——
7	IV	Looks like face of a rhinoceros or something.				
		Eyes, tusks.	——	——	——	——
8	IV	Nice crown.				
		Because of the way it's shaped.	——	——	——	——
9	I	All of it looks like a mask, cat face.				
		Grinning cat face mask, ears, eyes, mouth.	——	——	——	——
10	V	Man's head.	——	——	——	——

Ex. No.	Card No.		Loc.	Det.	Con.	P-O
11	III	Kidneys.				
		Shape of kidneys.	___	___	___	___
12	IX	< Face.				
		Man.	___	___	___	___
13	IX	∨ Middle section looks like an umbrella tree.				
		Color nothing to do with it.	___	___	___	___
14	III	Butterfly in center, wings and body .				
		I can't say what else.	___	___	___	___
15	X	∨ Two dogs.				
		That's all.	___	___	___	___
16	X	Pair of eyeglasses.				
		Don't have any temples.	___	___	___	___
17	IX	Small dog.	___	___	___	___
18	X	Crabs.				
		Shape and appendages.	___	___	___	___
19	VIII	Phallic symbol.				
		Length and shape.	___	___	___	___
20	VII	Sex symbol down here.	___	___	___	___
21	IX	Antlers.				
		Deer antlers.	___	___	___	___
22	IX	Fingers.	___	___	___	___
23	I	Legs of woman with heavy thighs coming down.	___	___	___	___
24	I	Might even be a mask.				
		Two eyes, cheeks; these fit around the ears.	___	___	___	___

Ex. No.	Card No.		Loc.	Det.	Con.	P-O
25	VII	Cacti.				
		Only outline.	——	——	——	——

Consult Form Scores Picture Sheet B

26	I	A big bat [whole].				
		Wings, body, antenna.	——	——	——	——
27	II	Long lower lip, the mouth with protruding lips.				
		Ubangi lips.	——	——	——	——
28	II	Butterfly, shape only, the body here.	——	——	——	——
29	X	Looks like a maze of sea animals, crabs, spiders. Shape only [whole].	——	——	——	——
30	II	Central part looks like some sort of urn or a vase or something like that.				
		Fan-shaped vase.	——	——	——	——
31	IV	Looks like a skate, a variety of fish belonging to shark family with sucker in front [whole].				
		Fish with big winglike structures.	——	——	——	——
32	VIII	Back of skull.				
		Back of skull, open areas.	——	——	——	——
33	VIII	Rock.				
		Just little extensions here, shaped like ones I've seen in park.	——	——	——	——
34	VIII <	Head of alligator with slit eyes.				
		Just head of alligator.	——	——	——	——
35	IX	Animal's head.				
		A deer's head.	——	——	——	——

Ex. No.	Card No.		Loc.	Det.	Con.	P-O
36	VIII	On top a mountain peak.				
		It seems so big.	___	___	___	___
37	II	Antennae of insect here.				
		Forward portion of insect, doesn't fit into any standard category. Rather strange.	___	___	___	___
38	VII	Shape inside a heart effect, a real heart.	___	___	___	___
39	VI	A turtle with lots of head.				
		A dead turtle with lots of heads, shell may be folded over—no.	___	___	___	___
40	X	Two acorns.				
		Just seems that way.	___	___	___	___
41	X	Rabbit's head.				
		Long ears.	___	___	___	___
42	III	∨ Some sort of animal there.				
		Something like a bull's head.	___	___	___	___
43	V	Claws, something to grab something with.	___	___	___	___
44	V	∨ Pair of pliers.	___	___	___	___
45	VI	> Resembles a ship, battleship.				
		No keel, mast, deck-gun sticking out.	___	___	___	___
46	III	Pair of hands.				
		Just the light gray part, ladies' hands.	___	___	___	___
47	III	The red in middle looks like a brassiere.				
		Just shape.	___	___	___	___

Ex. No.	Card No.		Loc.	Det.	Con.	P-O
48	III	Sea horse for good luck.				
		Long tail, shape only.	___	___	___	___
49	II	Something like a butterfly.				
		Looks exactly like one, body and wings.	___	___	___	___
50	II	Skate in middle, ocean fish.				
		Shape, tail coming out.	___	___	___	___

Consult Form Scores Picture Sheet C

Ex. No.	Card No.		Loc.	Det.	Con.	P-O
51	VI	A sting ray, kind of fish [whole].				
		Eyes on bottom and wings and stinger in back, where it is on fish.	___	___	___	___
52	II	Back of rabbit's ears.				
		Two ears back of rabbit's head.	___	___	___	___
53	V	Bat with rodent-like ears.				
		Wings, ears, tail-like structure.	___	___	___	___
54	VI	Land formation like France with English Channel. I don't know why I thought of channel.	___	___	___	___
55	VIII	Pancreas and kidneys.				
		The way they are in the body.	___	___	___	___
56	V	Rear legs of horse.				
		The hoof here.	___	___	___	___
57	IV	The whole thing looks like an insect.				
		Wings here, head could be here or here.	___	___	___	___
58	VI	Teeth.				
		Animals.	___	___	___	___

Ex. No.	Card No.		Loc.	Det.	Con.	P-O
59	I	A bell.	___	___	___	___
60	VIII	Starts as the shirt of a man, then here are his arms and going up to his collar [whole].				
		I don't think I was right.	___	___	___	___
61	IV ∨	On either side looks like two reptiles of some sort.	___	___	___	___
62	VII	Butterfly [whcle].				
		Just seems that way, these could be the wings.	___	___	___	___
63	IV ∨	Woman's shoe, heel.				
64	IV	Hind legs of a kitten.	___	___	___	___
65	IV	Duck's head and neck.	___	___	___	___
66	VI	Pussycat whiskers.				
		Just whiskers.	___	___	___	___
67	I	Woman's figure without a head.				
		Belted with bustle, bust, an incomplete manikin.	___	___	___	___
68	I	Dodecanese Islands, a map, association of islands around Turkey and Greece.	___	___	___	___
69	III	Penis.				
		Maybe an animal penis, monkey.	___	___	___	___
70	VII	Spain, The Bay of Biscay, Gibraltar, the top of Africa and the Suez.				
		Map of area, the shapes	___	___	___	___
71	VII	Kerosene lamp with a stand down here.	___	___	___	___

Ex. No.	Card No.		Loc.	Det.	Con.	P-O
72	V	This central portion, women with huge pompadours; they are peculiar.				
		Elongated head.	___	___	___	___
73	V	Crocodile head.	___	___	___	___
74	X	Wishbone.	___	___	___	___
75	VII ∨	Elephants' heads, eyes, trunk.				
		Head of elephant, trunk here.	___	___	___	___

3. Definition and Samples of the Movement Score

Movement scores imply the projection onto the blot of human or animal action or sense of aliveness, and the movement of natural forces, inanimate forces, and mechanical forces. Movement responses are scored: M, FM, m (Fm, mF, m).

   a. Human Movement (M) signifies the perception of human-like action or a posture which implies a projection of movement.

   M score is also used in the following instances:
   1. Human-like action attributed to a portion of a figure.
   2. Caricatures and statues in human-like action.
   3. Facial expressions.
   4. Animals in human-like action.

Card I	Here is Santa Claus hurrying along with a tree under his arm (D2).
Card IV	A giant with tremendous feet coming at me (W).
Card II	Two bears toasting each other, mugs raised (W).
Card III	Couple of men bowing to each other (W).
Card II	A war statue of two soldiers in hand-to-hand combat (W).
Card V <	Two men sleeping on hillside peacefully snoring (D1).
Card IX	A man with a cigarette in his mouth (D4). I just see the head; he is puffing hard on the cigarette.
Card VII	Two women with sassy expressions (W). Heads turned, lips pursed, hair up.

b. Animal Movement (FM) implies the perception of an animal form which is seen in animal-like action or in a posture that implies life.

Card V	A bat with wings outspread (W) Looks like he's flying.
Card VI	A dragonfly buzzing around (D2).
Card II	Two dogs rubbing noses (W).
Card IV	< A dog sitting on his haunches waiting for a command (D3).
Card III	A butterfly. It looks like it's ready to alight on a flower (D1).

c. Inanimate movement (m) implies the perception of natural or mechanical forces and abstract or symbolic forces. Inanimate movement responses are scored: Fm, mF, m.

(1) Form Inanimate Movement (Fm) implies perception of inanimate movement in a concept which has a definite and recognizable shape.

Card X	Like a parachute dropping earthward; something seems to be attached to it (D5).
Card VI	A rocket shooting off its runway (D3).
Card VIII	Flags waving in the breeze (D4).
Card III	A dead cat falling down (D2).
Card I	A hand in symbolic prayer (d3).

(2) Inanimate Movement Form (mF) implies the perception of inanimate movement in combination with form where the shape is vague or variable.

Card VI	Exploding fireworks (D2).
Card IX	A fountain spray—like water shooting (Center between lateral green-orange).
Card VII	Two rocks precariously balanced on a ledge (W). They seem about to fall.

(3) Inanimate Movement (m) implies the perception of inanimate movement alone or in a concept which has no shape.

Card IV	Confusion—turmoil—just looks like a lot of conflicting forces (W).
Card IX	Like everything ascending from Hell below (W).
Card VIII	This is Hell and Heaven on top and here are the forces keeping them apart (W).

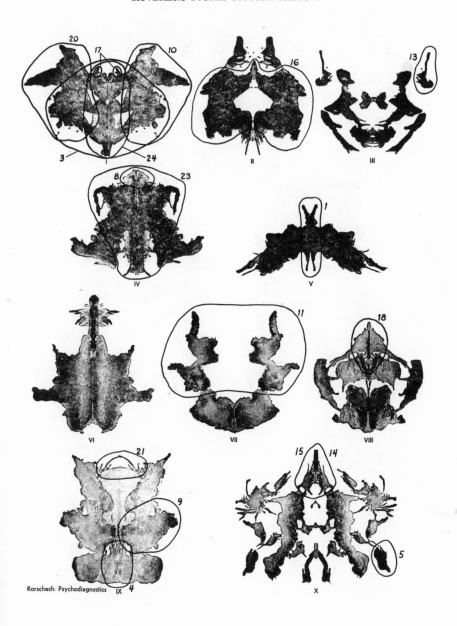

Rorschach: Psychodiagnostics

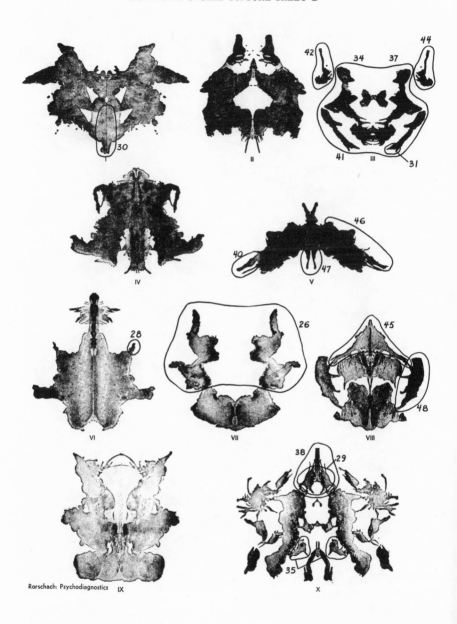

Rorschach: Psychodiagnostics

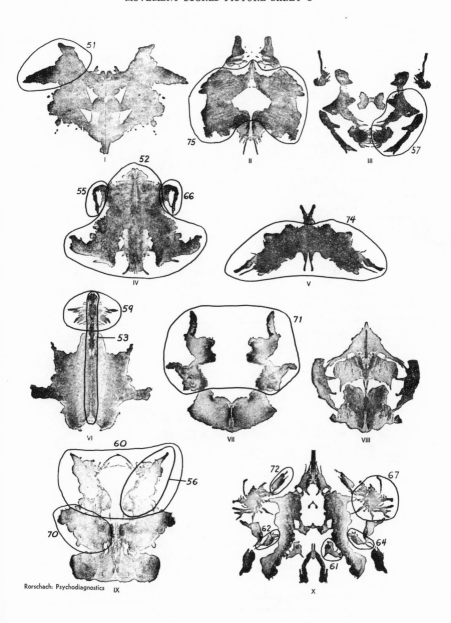

Rorschach: Psychodiagnostics

Ex. No.	Card No.		Loc.	Det.	Con.	P-O

Consult Movement Scores Picture Sheet A

1	V	Jack Rabbit.				
		Jack rabbit standing on hind legs.	—	—	—	—

2	I	Elephants with big ears [whole].				
		Legs, nose, standing on something.	—	—	—	—

3	I	A face.				
		Weird looking, as though leering.	—	—	—	—

4	IX	Sexual intercourse, penis, female organs present, buttocks, anus.				
		Penis, female organs, anus all present, sexual intercourse.	—	—	—	—

5	X	Reindeer or dogs.				
		Jumping.	—	—	—	—

6	VII	Looks like a lady looking in mirror [whole].				
		See both sides.	—	—	—	—

7	V	Looks like Mephistopheles with horns and feet ensconced in a flowing cape [whole].				
		Horns, back of his head, feet, arms holding out huge cape.	—	—	—	—

8	IV	A flower opening out, budding.				
		Can see the tightly curled center, the outer portion slowly opening, unfurling, looks like these slow motion films they make of plant action.	—	—	—	—

9	IX	< Figure climbing upon incline.				
		Has a walking stick, bushy hair.	—	—	—	—

Ex. No.	Card No.		Loc.	Det.	Con.	P-O
10	I	Bears sitting on their hind legs facing in opposite direction.				
		Paws out like this, fur hanging down (just edges), head looks up in air, here the haunches, hind leg haunches.	——	——	——	——
11	VII	This resembles two figures in argument, or a modern dance form, arms outstretched, look more like modern dance form. I don't like arguments.				
		Could be kneeling. This is the typical pose.	——	——	——	——
12	VI	Looks like a cat sitting up on its haunches with head all the way up and his whiskers up there [whole].	——	——	——	——
13	III	Creatures flying along because of some force.				
		Flowing robes, flying, probably pushed by the wind, could be saints.	——	——	——	——
14	X	Sad creature looking the situation over, like rabbit in Alice in Wonderland.				
		Walt Disney.	——	——	——	——
15	X	Two crickets sassing each other.	——	——	——	——
16	II	Two men squatting doing a folk dance, sort of a Russian dance.				
		Squatting hands up, knees, heads, disappear.	——	——	——	——
17	I	Happy little clowns looking at each other.				
		Bald, grotesque, gleeful clowns, like tall hats, faces sticking out, playful.	——	——	——	——

Ex. No.	Card No.		Loc.	Det.	Con.	P-O
18	VIII	Leering face of a pirate, a weird head.	___	___	___	___
19	II	Could be a couple of clowns with awful funny faces. They seem to be clapping hands [whole].	___	___	___	___
20	I	The outer figures look like two knights extending their.... either dueling or something of the sort.				
		In battle dress, like dueling (imitated posture).	___	___	___	___
21	IX	These things in middle look like cannons firing across ocean, anti-aircraft guns.				
		I can see the projectiles going.	___	___	___	___
22	II	Two bears dancing [whole].				
		Paws.	___	___	___	___
23	IV ∨	Looks like caterpillars climbing up a tree.				
		Caterpillars, the dark sides, the tree in the center and the side extensions are tree branches.	___	___	___	___
24	I	Two girls folk dancing with their hands up in the air.				
		Breasts, hips, hands up, skirts cover their feet, no heads.	___	___	___	___
25	V ∨	Rough drawing of a bomber falling down to earth [whole].				
		Bomber would be without a fusilage.	___	___	___	___

Consult Movement Scores Picture Sheet B

26	VII	Looks like two dogs up here.				
		With large ears; they seem sort of scared of each other; seem to want to run away and turning away.	___	___	___	___

Ex. No.	Card No.		Loc.	Det.	Con.	P-O
27	I	A woman with head cut off and two gentlemen at her side that look like ghosts [whole].				
		Men pulling away from each other, dress seen, neck supposed to be here and these are her hands.	——	——	——	——
28	VI	A foot.				
		Man's foot, sticking up, might be a man in there but don't really see it.	——	——	——	——
29	X	Two bulls.				
		Sort of horns, open mouths, sort of sitting down like.	——	——	——	——
30	I	A single woman, buttocks.				
		Back toward us, standing up.	——	——	——	——
31	III	Hands pointing with index finger.				
		Don't belong to these men.	——	——	——	——
32	IV	Looks like a bat [whole].				
		Head and wings, like sleeping.	——	——	——	——
33	X	Leaves falling down to earth [whole].				
		Slowly sifting down, just the shapes of different kinds of leaves, maybe distorted by the wind as they are falling.	——	——	——	——
34	III	Two kangeroos pulling at something.				
		Head and feet.	——	——	——	——
35	X	Dancers stretched out on floor in costume.				
		Dancers resting on arm, stretched out on floor.	——	——	——	——

Ex. No.	Card No.		Loc.	Det.	Con.	P-O
36	IX	An explosive center, forms floating around the calm after the storm [whole].	___	___	___	___
37	III	Looks like two men holding a package and putting it down.	___	___	___	___
38	X	Two boys crawling up a pole on top.	___	___	___	___
39	I	A spinning mechanism [whole]. These are spinning around the center. Could be some kind of elaborate top or toy mechanism; no idea of what the figures are because they spin so fast.	___	___	___	___
40	V	Couple of horses with elongated faces scooting out of thing; looks like Picasso horses. Jaw out, foreleg coming out rushing out at great speed almost horizontal.	___	___	___	___
41	III	Two birds dressed up; looks like carrying a basket. Face of a bird, basket they're carrying.	___	___	___	___
42	III	Sperm with tail going. Long tail.	___	___	___	___
43	V	Insect with antennae flying with back to us, long legs [whole]. Wings out flying.	___	___	___	___
44	III	∨ Monkey up in a tree looking down, tail hanging down, feet here.	___	___	___	___
45	VIII	Actively enclosing and protecting quality about the top. Comes down over other structures, coming down over.	___	___	___	___

Ex. No.	Card No.		Loc.	Det.	Con.	P-O
46	V	Female figure diving or swimming, not too clear.				
		Arm bent, body in motion, female leg.	___	___	___	___
47	V	∨ Snakes ready to come up.				
		Snakes head up, ready to come up.	___	___	___	___
48	VIII	A beaver, another beaver.				
		Shape and head, climbing.	___	___	___	___
49	I	Bat [whole].				
		Bat in flight, wings spread out, attached to body.	___	___	___	___
50	II	Could be an explosion, everything blown up.				
		The center of the explosion is always calm, but the rest is full of action. Could be an oil drum or gas tank exploding.	___	___	___	___

Consult Movement Scores Picture Sheet C

Ex. No.	Card No.		Loc.	Det.	Con.	P-O
51	I	Birds perched, wings out, up.				
		Birds perched wings up.	___	___	___	___
52	IV	These two look like feet, here head or tail of an animal.				
		Animal's feet and legs, half of an animal standing up that way.	___	___	___	___
53	VI	Something erupting, maybe a penis throwing off sperm or something with tender feelings is sticking out, tender on top with lot of eruption underneath.				
		Soft feelers, eruption underneath the surface.	___	___	___	___

Ex. No.	Card No.		Loc.	Det.	Con.	P-O
54	VII	Can-can girls [whole]. Can-can dances, head back, arms, legs, skirt.	___	___	___	___
55	IV	Drooping flowers. Drooping flowers or leaves, looks like dying flowers.	___	___	___	___
56	IX	A man leaning back balancing something, a juggler act. Head, body, hat, balancing hands out.	___	___	___	___
57	III ∨	Grotesque human figure. Eyes, nose, jowls, hair fluffy, hands shoulders, bent backwards like this.	___	___	___	___
58	X	Whole picture, some kind of philosophic aspirations of animal kingdom [whole]. Pervasive feeling, all animals engaged in aspiration and struggle.	___	___	___	___
59	VI	Top part looks like a bird sitting on something.	___	___	___	___
60	IX	Two little Santa Claus-like men carrying packs. Robes, packs, general shape.	___	___	___	___
61	X	Dwarfs or fairies. Head, with cap on, floating around in air.	___	___	___	___
62	X	Deer in flight. Deer antlers, body in flight.	___	___	___	___
63	V	Looks like a dancer with very fat legs, pigeon-toed and knock-kneed and big costume [whole].	___	___	___	___

Ex. No.	Card No.		Loc.	Det.	Con.	P-O
64	X	A couple of spiders pushing them (previously called leprechauns) closer together.				
		Pushing against leprechauns.	——	——	——	——
65	IV	Man's nose, his arms, his feet, silly hat on top and this might be something he's sitting on [whole].				
		Stump, not really, looks like he's sort of old.	——	——	——	——
66	IV	Woman's body doing a swan dive, with a man's head.	——	——	——	——
67	X	Two angry octupus men looking mad.				
		Looking very angry, arms out and up.	——	——	——	——
68	IV	∨ Sexual intercourse [whole].				
		Heads combined, no bodies, so united, just general feeling, legs dominant, symbolic of sexual organism.	——	——	——	——
69	II	Could be a statue depicting a toast.				
		Putting thin glasses up together [whole].	——	——	——	——
70	IX	A carving of an animal climbing on side of mountain.	——	——	——	——
71	VII	Two little boys looking very nasty.				
		Feather stuck in hair, eyes, noses.	——	——	——	——
72	X	Two lambs, young ones spring up.				
		Looks like lambs jumping.	——	——	——	——

Ex. No.	Card No.		Loc.	Det.	Con.	P-O
73	I	Two people and fountain in middle [whole].				
		Two people on side because of way it is shaped, bowl on top and water comes up through here. People come to get water.	___	___	___	___
74	V	Two buffaloes in a fight.	___	___	___	___
75	II	Looks like two figures in some sort of a dance in animal costume; they could be dressed as bears or rabbits; here are the ears.				
		Hands up there, head back, arm raised up [E. questioned whether they were male or female figures, S replied they just look like rabbits].	___	___	___	___

4. Definition and Samples of the Color Score

    Color responses indicate the use of color alone, or in combination with the formal aspects of areas selected in the formation of a concept. Color responses are differentiated into chromatic and achromatic color.

    Chromatic color responses imply the use of red, brown, green, and other bright colored areas, either alone or in combination with the formal aspects of the areas selected. Achromatic color responses imply the use of black, gray or white as surface color, either alone or in combination with the formal aspects of the areas selected. Chromatic color responses are scored: FC, CF, C, F/C, C/F; achromatic color responses are scored: FC', C'F, C'.

    a. The Chromatic Color Score

        (1) Form Color (FC) signifies the use of the color of the blot as part of a concept which has a definite and well-recognized shape. In FC responses the perceived color is the color usually associated with the concept.

Card III	A nice red hair ribbon bow (D1).
Card VIII	This part looks like a red rose. Here are the petals (D6).
Card II	It's a very beautiful butterfly—a red one (D1).
Card X	Blue birds flying toward each other (D8).
Card IX	Witches dressed up in colorful costume (D2).

(2) <u>Color Form</u> (CF) implies the use of color in a concept where the form is vague or variable.

<u>Card II</u>	These are blood stains (D2).
<u>Card X</u>	A beautiful garden in springtime with paths, trees, and flowers (W).
<u>Card VIII</u>	A piece of blue material (D4).
<u>Card IX</u>	Fire, glow and sparks (W).
<u>Card II</u>	A modernistic painting (W).

(3) <u>Pure Color</u> (C) indicates the use of color alone in the formation of the concept. The C score may be further subdivided as follows: Color Naming Score (Cn) signifies that the color as such was named; Color Description Score (Cdes) signifies that the color was merely a description and was not an elaboration of an FC or CF response; Color Symbolism Score (Csym) signifies that the color was used as a symbolic representation of an idea or feeling.

<u>Card X</u>	These are just colors, red, blue, green, brown (W).
<u>Card VIII</u>	All this reminds me of the colors in the West—it makes you feel gay (W).
<u>Card III</u>	Just blood—that's all (D2).
<u>Card IX</u>	Sky like when it's greenish blue (D1).
<u>Card II</u>	This red part reminds me of hell (D1).
<u>Card X</u>	Pretty pastel shades (W).

(4) <u>Forced Color</u> (F/C and C/F) implies the use of color in an arbitrary way in a concept with a definite and well-recognized shape (F/C) or in a concept where the form is vague or variable (C/F).

<u>Card VIII</u>	The internal organs of a person, the lungs here, stomach and intestines and here, the rib casing—like you see in an anatomy book (W).
<u>Card IX</u>	This is a map of the Scandinavian countries; the green is Norway and the orange is Sweden (side green and orange).
<u>Card X</u>	Blue crabs even though there are no blue crabs, but these are blue (D1).
<u>Card VIII</u>	Could be the inside of the body—just any part (W).
<u>Card IX</u>	Looks like a map where the colors are used for the different countries (W).

b. The Achromatic Color Score

   (1) <u>Form Achromatic Color</u> (FC') implies the use of white, gray, or black, as part of a con-

cept which has a definite and well-recognized shape.

Card V	Just glancing, a bat. The wings are spread out; it looks like a black bat (W).
Card VII	A lonely gray poodle dog (D4).
Card II	This is one of those white globes used in a kitchen (S).
Card V	Two animals up here. They look like little gray squirrels (d3).

(2) Achromatic Color Form (C'F) implies the use of white, gray or black, as part of a concept which has a vague or variable form.

Card IX	Like a mound of white clean snow (center area).
Card VII	Like smoke—gray smoke going up this way (W).
Card I	Like a picture of the heavens; the light and dark parts are crater masses because of the dark shadows (D2).

(3) Pure Achromatic Color (C') implies the use of white, gray, or black alone in the formation of a concept. As in the case of the C scores, C' scores also include responses where the color, black, gray, or white, is named (C'n); where the color is described (C'des); or where the color is used as symbolic of an idea or feeling (C'sym).

Card V	Like a nightmare because it's so black (W).
Card I	It's a sky, a strange grayness; not real sky, just a picture of a sky (W).
Card V	Day and night because of the black and white (W,S).

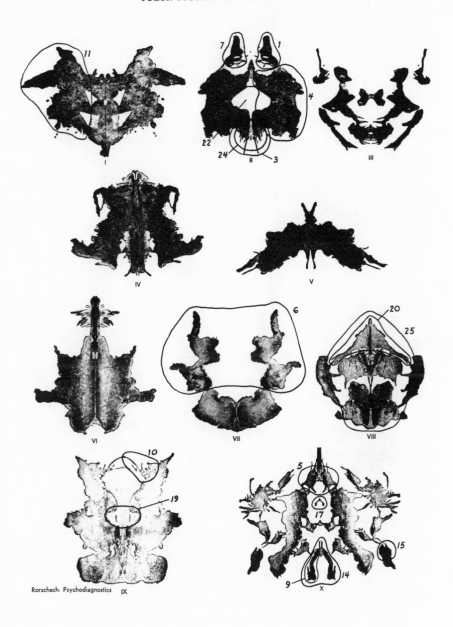

Rorschach: Psychodiagnostics

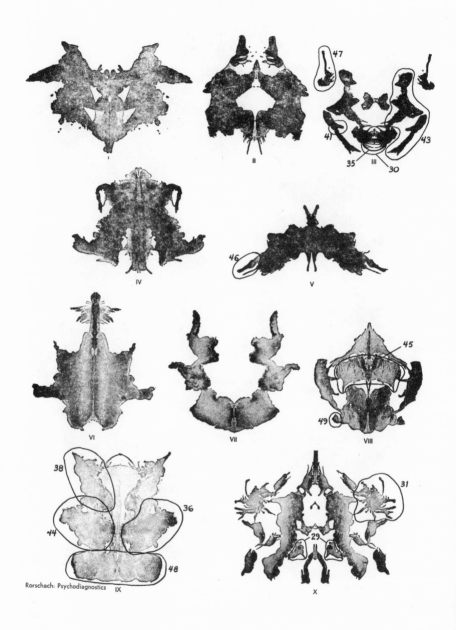

Rorschach: Psychodiagnostics

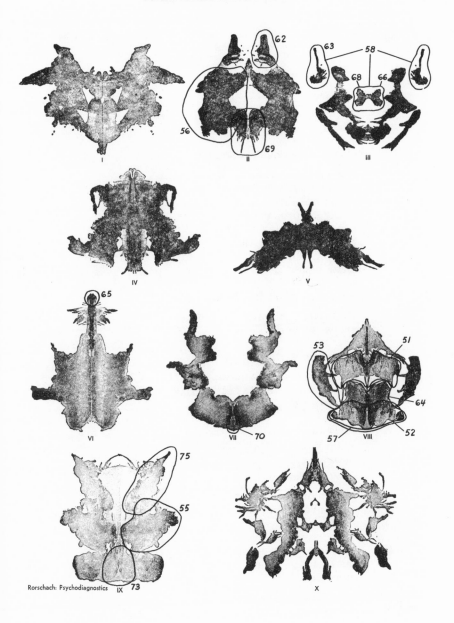

Rorschach: Psychodiagnostics

Ex. No.	Card No.		Loc.	Det.	Con.	P-O

Consult Color Scores Picture Sheet A

1   II   Red ankle socks.

A child's socks, just the color and shape.   ___ ___ ___ ___

2   IX   ∨ Looks like a bush [whole].

Here's the root or trunk and bush comes down like this, covered with dirt—that's what makes it orange brown and this is green because it has no sunlight and dirt hasn't reached it and reddish color is from sun burning it—the way the trunk comes down and colors.   ___ ___ ___ ___

3   II   Butterfly, right in middle.

Two things sticking up in air, shape, color.   ___ ___ ___ ___

4   II   Black smoke smudges.

Dark smudges of smoke, all that remains after a heavy fire, like oil burning.   ___ ___ ___ ___

5   X   Field mice.

Small and grayish color.   ___ ___ ___ ___

6   VII   Grey toy terriers.

The color of terriers and the faces are shaped like some I've seen.   ___ ___ ___ ___

7   II   Also looks like roosters—or chickens or fowl—I don't know much about that.

Red stuff hanging down and on top —puts me in mind of a rooster's comb but actually it doesn't look like a rooster.   ___ ___ ___ ___

Ex. No.	Card No.		Loc.	Det.	Con.	P-O
8	IV	These are such intense shades of grey [whole].				
		The greys vary here and get so intense they are almost black. The top seems to lighten and give it focus.	___	___	___	___
9	X	Looks like grass.				
		Because it's green and looks like weeds.	___	___	___	___
10	IX	Sea food—can see in restaurants with claws.				
		Lobsters—claws and color—may not have nails like that.	___	___	___	___
11	I	Two nuns with white surplice, heads here, and black garb.	___	___	___	___
12	X	What a happy picture. The colors of springtime and rebirth [whole].				
		Starting with the grey remains of last year, everything becomes alive again and there is the rosy tint of renewed hope.	___	___	___	___
13	VIII	Looks like inside of your body [whole].				
		I saw colored pictures like that—like a stomach or your sides.	___	___	___	___
14	X	Green things decoration.				
		Just color decoration.	___	___	___	___
15	X	Brownish color of head of airdale.	___	___	___	___
16	X	Could be a meadow [whole].				
		Because it has so many colors.	___	___	___	___
17	X	Pawn shop, three balls.				
		It's gold.	___	___	___	___

Ex. No.	Card No.		Loc.	Det.	Con.	P-O
18	VII	Grey shadows on a field of snow [space, whole].				
		You might be in the country and see this after a heavy snowfall.	___	___	___	___
19	IX	A sunrise.				
		Sunrise, varied colors.	___	___	___	___
20	VIII	Grey fungus mass.				
		Amorphous like a fungus, they are almost colorless.	___	___	___	___
21	V	The white space gives me the feeling of wide open spaces, freedom.				
		It can be avoided. You can always run away so that it doesn't hit you in the eye.	___	___	___	___
22	II	White cotton ball.				
		Cotton is generally that shape, I think.	___	___	___	___
23	IX	Flames [whole].				
		Bottom red and top orange—mostly in orange are flames. Green—never saw green flames but once I did, one little spark.	___	___	___	___
24	II	Female sex organs.				
		This would suggest it because of narrow opening and this would also be the womb, the color makes it look like diagrams in a book.	___	___	___	___
25	VIII	Looks like the frame of the body— the chest, the stomach, the ribs and the tubes running into the lungs.				
		Body not actually constructed that way—color—very often in anatomy books.	___	___	___	___

Ex. No.	Card No.		Loc.	Det.	Con.	P-O

Consult Color Scores Picture Sheet B

26	VII	These are lots of greys [whole]. This is light grey. Then it gets darker. And here it's black and this is white.	___	___	___	___
27	VIII	Human body and visceral detail [whole]. An anatomical drawing, center of bony structure, visceral areas demarcated in color, lungs, stomach and lower organs.	___	___	___	___
28	X	A formal garden in spring with an iron fence at the end two banks of pink azaleas [whole]. Pink azaleas, clumps of blue, yellow and brown iris around the central pink shrubs.	___	___	___	___
29	X	A few eggs dropped around here and some splashed here.	___	___	___	___
30	III	Grey and white matter of spinal cord.	___	___	___	___
31	X	Like Chinese animals, scorpion. We have a tapestry at home has Chinese dragon, here face and eye—and it is blue.	___	___	___	___
32	VI	Mostly an interesting study in grey [whole]. There are various shades of grey, black and white placed to make a pleasing pattern. See—here it is black, then below it's white and to the sides are various greys.	___	___	___	___
33	IX	Just a mass of color, could be a coat of arms or an ad of something [whole].	___	___	___	___

Ex. No.	Card No.		Loc.	Det.	Con.	P-O

34   IX   It might be undersea coral [whole].

Some sort of vegetation—partly the color. And these little streamers and stuff.   ___   ___   ___   ___

35   III   Icicles.

Color and shape— hanging in same direction.   ___   ___   ___   ___

36   IX   Beautiful green ball dress.

Lovely green evening dress lying ready to be worn, skirt spread so it won't get crushed.   ___   ___   ___   ___

37   VIII   Seaweed or wild plant [whole].

Mostly the color, some sort of underwater flowering plant.   ___   ___   ___   ___

38   IX   Could get little Santa Claus hanging on a Christmas tree.

Crudely done face—back with toy pack—Color part of idea, color leads to illusion.   ___   ___   ___   ___

39   IV   It looks like ink spilled on a piece of paper [whole].   ___   ___   ___   ___

40   IX   Reminds me of anatomy picture— perhaps of a human body—like physiology classroom—insides open up describing different sections of torso. Green reminds me of gall—gall bladder— lower red some muscular formation. Orange seems to be the chest—vertebra running down the middle [whole].   ___   ___   ___   ___

41   III   Baby's booties.

The color makes it look like that.   ___   ___   ___   ___

Ex. No.	Card No.		Loc.	Det.	Con.	P-O
42	II	Medical charts, part of an anatomical chart [whole].				
		You see the veins, different muscles, veins are usually in red.	___	___	___	___
43	III	These are black and white.				
		Here it's black, then white, then black, then the white space, then more black.	___	___	___	___
44	IX	The sea.				
		Color of green.	___	___	___	___
45	VIII	Blue sky.				
		Color of sky blue.	___	___	___	___
46	V	Dead wood of trees, dead wood branches.				
		White dead bare branches.	___	___	___	___
47	III	Blood.				
		A blood splotch.	___	___	___	___
48	IX	Two pink creatures, with heads facing away from each other, human.				
		Foetus, pink color.	___	___	___	___
49	VIII ∨	Brown spaniels, English spaniels with floppy ears.				
		Part of body seen too.	___	___	___	___
50	IX	This is a watercolor exercise perhaps [whole].				
		Green in the center runs into the orange on top and blends with the pink below. They all blend and fuse in the center but spread out and are thinned with the white.	___	___	___	___

Ex. No.	Card No.		Loc.	Det.	Con.	P-O

Consult Color Scores Picture Sheet C

| 51 | VIII | Blue flags on a twin standard. | | | | |
| | | Flags just for decoration. | ___ | ___ | ___ | ___ |

| 52 | VIII | A butterfly. | | | | |
| | | Looks like four wings—body—different colored wings—mounted. | ___ | ___ | ___ | ___ |

| 53 | VIII | Looks a little like a carrot except not the right color. | ___ | ___ | ___ | ___ |

| 54 | VIII | This is creation. Here at the orange and red everything is beautiful. Then there is a space of trial and tribulation leading to a mellower period, then life becomes grayer. There is always something of joy on either side and even the end has a rosy tint [whole, space]. | ___ | ___ | ___ | ___ |

| 55 | IX | Pistachio ice cream. | | | | |
| | | No shape, it depends on how you dish it out. | ___ | ___ | ___ | ___ |

| 56 | II | A bear. | | | | |
| | | Shape, black bear, no real body. | ___ | ___ | ___ | ___ |

| 57 | VIII | Menstruation. | | | | |
| | | Color. | ___ | ___ | ___ | ___ |

| 58 | III | Red spots, decorative irrelevance. | | | | |
| | | Just decoration. | ___ | ___ | ___ | ___ |

| 59 | I | A butterfly [whole, space]. | | | | |
| | | It's a black and white one like you see sometimes. Head about here. | ___ | ___ | ___ | ___ |

Ex. No.	Card No.		Loc.	Det.	Con.	P-O

60   II   A problem in painting [whole].

Interested in what happens when you mix colors in painting, the intricate effect of black and red superimposed as contrasted to black and red above. It's a difficult problem.

           —— —— —— ——

61   VIII   There are a lot of bright colors here, red, blue, pink and orange [whole].

Here's red, pink, blue, orange.   —— —— —— ——

62   II   Red flames.

Just color and shape—don't know what it comes from. Sort of like flame of candle but don't see any candle here.

           —— —— —— ——

63   III   Chinese lanterns let down from strings, shape and color.

           —— —— —— ——

64   VIII   Piece of cloth, to be cut for clothing.

Possibly a taffeta of two colors, you know the way taffeta comes in related colors. This pink and orange will be a ladies' blouse.

           —— —— —— ——

65   VI   Head with eyes—almost like a ghost.

Something almost white about it— ghost face.

           —— —— —— ——

66   III   Could be a butterfly.

Looks more like a bow—has no butterfly. Put on your dress— dress bow—it's the color too!

           —— —— —— ——

67   X   What a lot of colors, pink and yellow and blue and green [whole].

Pink, green, blue, yellow, gold, brown, grey, just about every color I can think of.

           —— —— —— ——

Ex. No.	Card No.		Loc.	Det.	Con.	P-O

68   III   Kidneys or adrenal glands.

Kidneys don't curve like that, also
not adrenal glands but associate
that shade with kidneys and kidneys
with glands. Color—life blood
through them.   ___ ___ ___ ___

69   II   Monkeys in the zoo.

Just their red behinds, ugly sort
of thing.   ___ ___ ___ ___

70   VII   Bottom looks like a little house.

White house.   ___ ___ ___ ___

71   I   Symbol of airman's death [whole].

Blackness and shape of insignia
make me think of airman's death.   ___ ___ ___ ___

72   IV   Black hair strewn all over bar-
ber's floor [whole].   ___ ___ ___ ___

73   IX   Baby's pink buttocks.

Pink like a baby.   ___ ___ ___ ___

74   VIII   Chalky pastel colors [whole].

Looks like pastel colors, just the
color quality.   ___ ___ ___ ___

75   IX   Norway here.

Colored map.   ___ ___ ___ ___

5. Definition and Samples of the Shading Score
   Shading responses indicate the use of the black, gray, and
white shading nuances of the blot in the formation of the concept. The shading nuances of the blot suggest surface and texture qualities, or depth, distance, and diffusion. It is along
these dimensions that the shading responses are differentiated.
   a. The Surface and Texture Score indicates the use of the
      shading nuances to suggest surface qualities; i.e., rough-
      ness or smoothness, roundness or carved effects, high-

lights on a polished surface, transparency, the projection of
color on the shaded portions of noncolored areas of the blot,
or the delineation of facial features or objects as a result
of the fine differentiation in the shading. Surface and texture
responses are scored: Fc, cF, c.

(1) Form Texture (Fc) implies the use of the shading
nuances of the blot to describe a surface impression
as part of a concept which has a definite and well-
recognized shape, or the use of shading nuances to
describe a finely differentiated texture effect, although the object may have indeterminate form.

Card II	This looks like the stuffed head and shoulders of a very furry bear (D3). It looks furry right through here.
Card II ∨	These red parts look like socks. The color is all wrong but the different shadings of the color make them look soft and wooly (D2).
Card IV	A bear skin with thick hair down the center (W).
Card X	A mythological animal carved out of rough stone—like a child would make (D4).
Card VI	The bottom part looks like a beautifully colored Indian blanket (D1). (Q) The different shades make me think of it.
Card VI	Like a highly polished bed post. You can see the highlights (D3).

(2) Texture Form (cF) implies the use of the shading
qualities to suggest surface impressions as part of
a concept which has a vague or variable shape.

Card V	A piece of meat wrapped in cellophane.
Card VII	The bottom part looks like a piece of granite. It has that rough feel (D1).
Card IX	This part looks like cotton candy that children buy at country fairs (D5).
Card VI	Could be a piece of fur from an animal —no particular kind (D1).

(3) Pure Texture (c) implies the use of the shading
qualities for surface impression without regard for
shape in the formation of a concept.

Card IV	Looks like a lot of mud—it's so messy (W).
Card VII	Like sand and gravel—the little dots over here (D1).
Card VII	The whole thing looks like a mess of cotton. It seems so soft (W).

b. <u>The Vista and Distance Scores</u> indicate the use of the shading qualities of the blot to suggest distance. Distance
   responses are scored: FK, Fk, kF, k.

   (1) <u>Vista</u> (FK) implies the use of shading to suggest
   distance between two objects or between two parts of
   an object.

<u>Card III</u>	Like a pelvis seen in a skeleton — these are the front ribs and these are the back ribs (D3).
<u>Card II</u>	Like a Chinese pagoda in the distance with a lake in front of it and bushes on the sides of the lake (W̌, S).
<u>Card IV</u>	On top here it looks like the partly open lips of a vagina. It's very well done with the darker part in the center suggesting depth (d2).
<u>Card VI</u>	Looks like part of an open book with the center depression here (dr).
<u>Card IV</u> >	Like a scene from across a river—here is the river and these could be tall mountains in the distance (W). Oh, all of it is reflected below.
<u>Card VI</u>	Most of this looks like a terrain as seen from a low-flying air-plane. You can see the hills and valleys (W).
<u>Card I</u>	A relief map (D2). You know, something you build out of clay to show mountains and valleys.
<u>Card II</u>	This looks like a cave (W̌, S). The black part is the outside of the cave and the white is the hole looking out.

  (2) <u>Representative Distance</u> (Fk, kF, k) implies the use
   of shading to suggest three dimensional expanse
   projected on a two-dimensional plane. This type of
   response is most frequently given as X-rays or
   topographical maps.

    (a) <u>Form Representative Distance</u> (Fk) implies the
   use of the shading to represent distance in a
   concept which has a definite and well-recognized
   shape.

Card III   Looks like an X-ray of a pelvic
           girdle (D3).

Card I   This looks like a topographical
           map of a section in Western
           Montana (dr).
           You know those maps where the
           darker shadings represent height
           and the lighter shadings depth.

(b) Representative Distance Form (kF) implies the
    use of the shading to represent distance in a
    concept which has a vague or variable shape.

Card II   Could be a topographical map
           of any country (D3).

Card VI   An X-ray of some part of the
           human body (dr).

(c) Pure Representative Distance (k) implies the
    use of shading to represent distance where
    form is disregarded altogether.

Card IV   Shading here makes me think of
           X-rays (dr).
           Has an X-ray quality, could be
           of anything.

Note: Small k's rarely occur without some
element of form.

c. The Diffusion Score indicates the use of the shading of the
blot to describe unorganized space-filling diffusion or expanse. Diffusion responses are scored: KF, K

(1) Diffusion Form (KF) implies the use of the shading
    qualities to describe unorganized, space-filling diffu-
    sion or expanse in which some shape is suggested.

Card II   Like smoke coming out of a
           chimney (D2).

Card IX   Looks like a fine spray of water,
           like when it's fanned out (center
           between lateral green, orange).

Card VII   This looks like cloud formation
           (W).

(2) Pure Diffusion(K) implies the use of the shading
    qualities of the blot to describe unorganized, space-
    filling diffusion or expanse in which no space is
    suggested.

Card IV   Looks very hazy; misty, like
           a fog maybe (W).

Card VII   Just clouds (W).
           Can't say anything more about
           them.

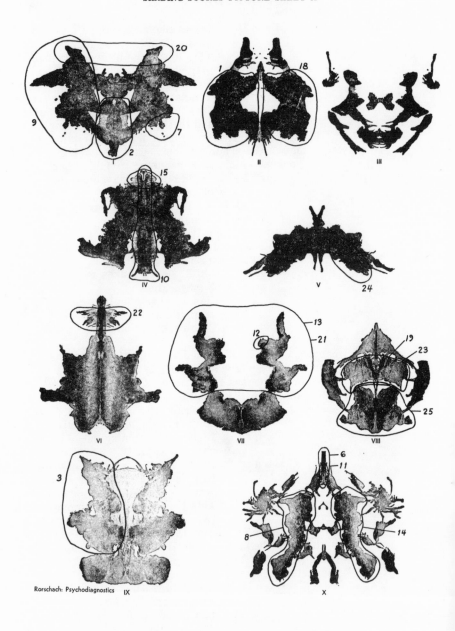

Rorschach: Psychodiagnostics

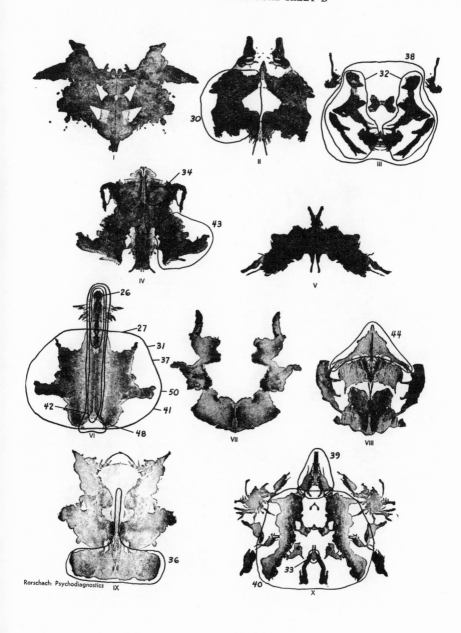

Rorschach: Psychodiagnostics

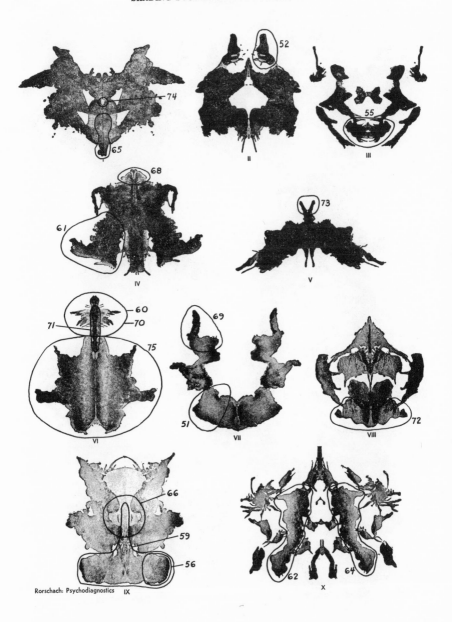

Rorschach: Psychodiagnostics

Ex. No.	Card No.		Loc.	Det.	Con.	P-O

Consult Shading Scores Picture Sheet A

1	II ∨	Two dogs, setters — with sort of French Poodle—like trimmings.				
		Long nose, little eyelash, mouth, neck, chest—from then on indistinct—frowsy hair like French Poodles but this is setter's face.	___	___	___	___
2	I	Spinal cord.				
		Different vertebrae, looks like picture in text, color not of living tissue, X-ray study.	___	___	___	___
3	IX	Looks something like mountains in the distance.				
		This [the green] looks near; this [the orange] looks far away.	___	___	___	___
4	VIII	Reflection in water [whole].				
		Beautiful reflection—very far away. This is rock.	___	___	___	___
5	IV	I just respond in terms of a touching quality. I know I should try to make something of it [whole].				
		Would like to touch it, it's soft and maybe spongy.	___	___	___	___
6	X	Organ pipe roughly speaking.				
		It's round—has shading and light in the front.	___	___	___	___
7	I	Coastline with islands—fluoroscope feeling—light things on different level.				
		Map with areas built up to give altitude—fluoroscopic feeling from the different shades.	___	___	___	___

Ex. No.	Card No.		Loc.	Det.	Con.	P-O
8	X	These are just fossils. Big pieces of stone worn down by water.	___	___	___	___
9	I	Some parts look like it might be part of a map. Ocean here, kind you see in geography—usually colored or something else—these gray maps they show in books. Perhaps they resemble the topographical maps.	___	___	___	___
10	IV ∨	Central portion looks like stunted tree been cut off. Trunk of tree looks rough. Markings on bark—tropical trees—with extensions.	___	___	___	___
11	X	I see a face—very elongated—like Egyptian carved figure, eyes and nose, peculiar coiffure—carved in stone.	___	___	___	___
12	VII	Oklahoma. Some oil derricks are further than others.	___	___	___	___
13	VII	Gargoyles. Gargoyles in human shape look like in a cathedral, possibly of stone, rough surface of stone, also rounded effect.	___	___	___	___
14	X	Might be a plume for a woman's hat. It's fuzzy like that and this shading gives the effect of it—could be any shape.	___	___	___	___
15	IV	Looks like a shell I once found. Looks like the grain of shell. It's not so much the shape of the shell as the clear patterns of markings.	___	___	___	___

Ex. No.	Card No.		Loc.	Det.	Con.	P-O
16	VII	Basin in a mountain [whole, space].				
		Something like a valley and the rest are mountains—so rigid and uneven.	⎯	⎯	⎯	⎯
17	VII	Something like a canal [whole, space].				
		Land is gray. Like Panama (Canal) in dark part in center. Looks like a picture I saw recently.	⎯	⎯	⎯	⎯
18	II	Rams or lambs—cloven hoof—bison—something like that. Humpy animal—looks like buffalo.				
		Have very rough skin. I saw definite lines.	⎯	⎯	⎯	⎯
19	VIII	Shape of a pillow.				
		Except for color—gives you an idea of something round and soft. You can see the folds in here.	⎯	⎯	⎯	⎯
20	I	This looks like a cross-section of a lake been drained dry. Prehistoric rock.				
		Lake in white part—eroded down—just edge. These marks are strata—a stream or river.	⎯	⎯	⎯	⎯
21	VII	These clouds look like they might be people.				
		Look like clouds but vaguely remind me of a profile of a head.	⎯	⎯	⎯	⎯
22	VI	Top looks like a negative of a photograph of a brightly colored butterfly.				
		A butterfly. If in color it would be beautiful; this is a negative of a photograph.	⎯	⎯	⎯	⎯

Ex. No.	Card No.		Loc.	Det.	Con.	P-O
23	VIII	Pieces of cellophane held over water.	—	—	—	—
24	V	A storm cloud—because of its fullness.	—	—	—	—
25	VIII ∨	A valley. Rest of orange and red is sides for cars to pass through.	—	—	—	—

Consult Shading Scores Picture Sheet B

Ex. No.	Card No.		Loc.	Det.	Con.	P-O
26	VI	It looks like a little animal I studied in biology—pigmented body —two eye spots. See the alimentary canal.	—	—	—	—
27	VI	Scaly surface of some kind. Looks like it is a section of scales of some kind, shading makes it look like that. Just scales. No special kind.	—	—	—	—
28	VII	Cloudlike effect here [whole]. Seems three-dimensional.	—	—	—	—
29	IV	A photographic map like we used to get in the army. The center is a well-traveled path [whole]. There is a path, dense woods, and suggestions of side roads. I used to see aerial maps like this in the Army.	—	—	—	—
30	II	A rough furryness, animal-like. Looks like it would feel rough and furry—that is the major impression.	—	—	—	—
31	VI	All look like plains—like one of those maps—areas to represent different types of land, cultivated or high hilly areas. Part of a map perhaps.	—	—	—	—

Ex. No.	Card No.		Loc.	Det.	Con.	P-O

Ex. No.	Card No.		Loc.	Det.	Con.	P-O
32	III	Mountain and snow—reflected in water.				
		Sort of gulch—mountain ridge heavily wooded—like timber line. Distance darkness and depth— looks heavily wooded—gives depth.	___	___	___	___
33	X ∨	One window of a church or building lit with figure far away—indistinct.	___	___	___	___
34	IV	Spots on lungs, chest area.				
		Looks like X-ray showing spots in the lungs, there is a lack of clarity.	___	___	___	___
35	II	Looks like an X-ray of somebody's insides [whole].				
		Because of the line of bones.	___	___	___	___
36	IX ∨	This looks like a big umbrella tree.				
		Bushy and full—looks like foliage. Maybe umbrella tree—doesn't look like that—I never saw one.	___	___	___	___
37	VI	A piece of moldy bread.				
		Shading is mold forming on bread mass.	___	___	___	___
38	III	Looks like a cavern.				
		Jagged edges—I've seen pictures —enter in here—walls and empty area.	___	___	___	___
39	X	This looks like the bronchial tube and lungs.				
		Dark and light areas— the shading.	___	___	___	___

Ex. No.	Card No.		Loc.	Det.	Con.	P-O

40   X   Like a river.

Looking down on something, here a
dam and here is the land formation;
like a bridge across here, like
those moving railroad bridges and
this is the platform in the middle
of the river.   ___ ___ ___ ___

41   VI   Skin of animal on board, furry,
striped effect and paws.

Stretched out skin of animal, furry
texture, lines down back and on
legs.   ___ ___ ___ ___

42   VI   The plan or blueprint of cave with
passages.

See darker colors of walls— main
passage and other passage.   ___ ___ ___ ___

43   IV   Looks like a map of Italy, shadings
show mountains and terrain.

The map of Italy showing mountains and valley. I'm not sure
they're correct but they look like
that sort of map. I don't know the
name, it has a special name.   ___ ___ ___ ___

44   VIII Mountains in the distance, seems so
far away, especially the top part.   ___ ___ ___ ___

45   X   A fantastic shimmering scene
[whole].

Shimmery shining light off surface,
the effect of light.   ___ ___ ___ ___

46   IV   This looks like a very bad case of
tuberculosis shown in X-ray [whole,
space].

Arms droop off—lungs in middle—
can't see the ribs—that show per-
son has bad case of T.B.   ___ ___ ___ ___

Ex. No.	Card No.		Loc.	Det.	Con.	P-O
47	VII	Balls of cotton [whole].				
		Separated balls of cotton, soft and fluffy.	___	___	___	___
48	VI	Alimentary canal, double heart, a big spinal column, and feces.				
		An X-ray of alimentary canal, double heart, spinal column and feces.	___	___	___	___
49	VII	Rock formations [whole].				
		Rock masses, feels like rock.	___	___	___	___
50	VI	Photographic view from an airplane.				
		Here could be a ravine with plateau on two sides.	___	___	___	___

Consult Shading Scores Picture Sheet C

Ex. No.	Card No.		Loc.	Det.	Con.	P-O
51	VII	Scottie's head—ear, snout.				
		In form of chess piece resting on little stand—it is carved—you can see the highlights.	___	___	___	___
52	II	Red might look like snails from the swerve of the thing.				
		Swirl effect, laminated.	___	___	___	___
53	VI	A highway under construction. It's not finished—dug out of a hill [whole].				
		Down here is the finished road made into a valley—shading makes it look like a road deep in a valley—you're above looking down.	___	___	___	___
54	II	Thick smoke, sort of in a spiral—might have been a heavy oil fire [whole].				
		Smoke looks thick.	___	___	___	___

Ex. No.	Card No.		Loc.	Det.	Con.	P-O
55	III	Pelvic bony structure. Nice pelvis, shades of grey show which part further back—looks like textbook illustration.	——	——	——	——
56	IX	A portrait. Shaded here—looks like stone.	——	——	——	——
57	I	Looks like a cloud that you see that seems to look like something—this could be some kind of bird [whole]. Did you ever look at clouds and see things, sort of shapes? This looks like a bird, vaguely of course—it's really just a cloud.	——	——	——	——
58	VI	A photograph, a negative that has been ruined out of focus [whole]. Just the quality of a negative, shading, but doesn't look like anything.	——	——	——	——
59	IX	∨ The A-bomb cloud. The shape of the cloud of the A-bomb. Heavy smoke. You've seen the pictures.	——	——	——	——
60	VI	Red, yellow and purple butterfly. The different shades look like the different colors.	——	——	——	——
61	IV	A hammered piece of metal—the bumpy effect.	——	——	——	——
62	X	All have some relief map look.	——	——	——	——
63	V	Smoke spread out, looks like a smudge [whole].	——	——	——	——
64	X	Contour of mountains—looking far away—shading.	——	——	——	——

Ex. No.	Card No.		Loc.	Det.	Con.	P-O
65	I	Looks like some X-ray picture of something—light and dark shadows in it.				
		The torso of the body.	——	——	——	——
66	IX	A mist.				
		A mist, probably a fine morning mist like you see in the country, it may be clearing.	——	——	——	——
67	IV	Heavy smoke, not quite shaped like the A-bomb cloud [whole].				
		May be the smoke left from some kind of explosion.	——	——	——	——
68	IV	Etching of a fern or a design—it's very pretty.				
		The delicacy of an etching.	——	——	——	——
69	VII	Looks like animal with bushy tail—squirrel or something like that.	——	——	——	——
70	VI	Indian totem design.				
		You can see the different colors of the design.	——	——	——	——
71	VI	This looks like a brass post.				
		It looks as though it is so highly polished light is reflected off it.	——	——	——	——
72	VIII	This looks like a piece of tissue paper because of the way the light seems to come through it.				
		Just plain tissue paper	——	——	——	——
73	V	Either one of these things sticking up here looks like a piece of meat or bone wrapped in cellophane.				
		It looks the way it is in the market, packaged in cellophane. A leg of some kind of meat.	——	——	——	——

Ex. No.	Card No.		Loc.	Det.	Con.	P-O

74	I	This little hole in the middle looks like a knot hole that you look through in a fence to see the construction going on.				
		I can about make out the foundation of a building in the wide open space beyond it.	___	___	___	___
75	VI	This part looks like water, very deep sea.				
		It's not that I can look into it but it gives me the feeling of a mass of water.	___	___	___	___

C. Scoring Categories for Content of the Response

    1. General Meaning and Definition of the Content Score

        Content scores refer to <u>what</u> is seen. Content describes the associations of the subject as he perceives the blot material and fits names to what he sees. There is a limitless number of categories for content scores. The majority of responses fall within the three main classifications: humans (H), animals (A) and objects (obj). There are other categories such as food and clothing which are less frequently needed but are nevertheless important. The worker may find it necessary to develop categories on the basis of the responses he is required to score.

      a. The Human Score

        (1) <u>Whole Human</u> (H) implies the perception of a complete human figure or a major portion of it.

Card III	Two men in dress suits bowing to one another (W).
Card VII	Two ladies with elaborate hair combs talking to one another over a tea table (W).
	They are leaning forward gossiping.
Card X	Two dancers stretched out (D10).
	Wearing elaborate ruffled costumes.

        (2) <u>Human Detail</u> (Hd) signifies that only a portion of a human figure was seen.

Card II	Hands folded as though in prayer (d1).
Card V	Head of a man with a large nose, mustache and beard (D1).
	He has curly hair and mustache.

      Card III   Lower portion of 18th century gentle-
                   man (D5).
                   Kneebreeches, tight hose, and fancy high
                   heel shoes.

(3) Mythological or Caricature [(H)] signifies that the
human figure seen is not real, either in the sense that
a mythological figure or a caricature of a human figure
was perceived.

      Card IX   Witches (D2).
                   Tall pointed hats and loose gowns.
                   Their hands are stretched out, doing
                   evil.
      Card I   Santa Claus with a tree under his arm
                   (D2).
                   Pointed hat, bulky clothes, Christmas
                   tree under his arm.
      Card VIII   Evil ghost head (D3).
                   Ghost head looming out.
      Card X   Gargoyles (D9).
                   Grinning gargoyles carved in building.

b. The Animal Score

(1) Whole Animal (A) implies the perception of a complete animal figure or a major portion of it.

      Card X   Two caterpillars (D2).
                   Color and shape.
      Card VIII   Rats climbing up rocks; perhaps they
                   are some other kind of rodents (D1).
      Card II   Two circus bears performing, their
                   heads up, noses touching (D3).
      Card VII   A shaggy Scotch terrier (D4).
                   Sniffing something, ears up and tail out,
                   shaggy fur.

(2) Animal Detail (Ad) signifies that only a portion of an
animal figure was perceived.

      Card IV   Head of a bull (D1).
                   Horns, eyes and ears.
      Card IX   Lobster claws (d1).
                   Color and shape.
      Card III   A chicken's head (d2).
                   Scrawny neck.

(3) Animal Object (Aobj) signifies the perception of
objects made from animals or parts of animals.

      Card VI   Fur rug on a floor (W).
                   Animal skin on a floor, paws, head and
                   tail, furry, perhaps a bearskin.

        Card IX   A pair of antlers on the wall for decoration (d3).

                  A hunter's trophy. Just the antlers.

        Card IX   An animal skull (D7).

                  Seems to be dried by desert sun like in Georgia O'Keefe painting.

(4) Mythological Animal [(A)] signifies that the animal figure seen is not real or is engaged in unrealistic activity.

        Card X   Two rodents having an angry intellectual discussion (D4).

                  They are fighting about something very profound.

        Card V   A rabbit dressed in a flowing ballet costume (W).

                  It is up on its legs ready to perform.

c. Other Content Scores

(1) Object (Obj) implies the perception of a man-made object.

        Card II   A pair of red socks (D2).

                  Could be woolen socks; the tops are rolled down.

        Card III   A bow tie (D1).

                  Shape of bow tie.

        Card X   The three gold balls that are the pawnbrokers' sign—hang outside shops (D12).

        Card VIII   A pair of blue flags (D4).

                  They look like they are in the breeze, waving.

(2) Anatomy (At) implies the perception of anatomical concepts.

        Card III   Looks like a skeleton (D9).

                  Looks like a person's ribs.

        Card IX   Bottom of spinal column (dr).

                  Spinal column, vertebrae, segments.

        Card X   Human body rib section, an X-ray (D14).

                  X-ray of ribs and backbone.

        Card I   Looks like a steer, skull of a steer (W).

(3) Nature (N) implies the perception of natural landscape or topographical features seen in nature.

        Card VI   Rocky terrain and a canyon in the center (D1).

        Card II   A path in a forest (dr).

                  Heavily wooded forest with path in the center, trees overshadow it.

        Card VIII   A glowing sunset (D7).

                  Colors of sunset in the summer.

    Card V   Wooded mountains (W).
                    Lighter areas might be bare or rocky
                    parts like you sometimes see.

(4) Geography (Geo) topographical features seen as part
of a map or scientific representation.
    Card III   Map of Italy (D5).
                    Looks like boot the way Italy does.
    Card VII   A map of North and South America (D4).
                    Darker parts mean mountains.
    Card I   Islands in the Pacific (dd).
                    They are always scattered groups of
                    small islands; no particular group, just
                    small islands.

(5) Plant (Pl) signifies the perception of flowers or other
botanical concepts.
    Card VIII A rose (D2).
    Card X   Daffodils (D15).
    Card VI   ∨A tree (W).

(6) Art (Art) artistic technicalities or art forms as the
predominant concepts.
    Card IX   Modern painting (W).
                    Colors and shapes but no definite
                    meaning.
    Card VII   Carved statue of rock; part of it left
                    in natural rock form the way they some-
                    times do; could be heads of children (W).
    Card III   Modern background, like backdrop for
                    a play (W).
                    A jazz scene, colors of bright sharp
                    modern tempo.

(7) Abstract (Abs) ideational rather than concrete percepts.
    Card VI   Something spinning around very fast
                    a-whirling (W).
                    It's so fast, it looks like nothing; just
                    the whirling.
    Card VIII The pink is the evil which is slowly de-
                    stroying the good in the world (W).
                    Evil is triumphing and destroying the
                    good.

(8) Sex (Sex)
    Card VI   Like a penis—just this part (D3).
    Card V   Heavy breasts of a woman (dr).
    Card VII   This looks like the female genital and
                    the dark shading here makes it seem
                    like hair (d1).
    Card IX   Symbol of intercourse—penis and va-
                    gina (D8).

Rorschach: Psychodiagnostics

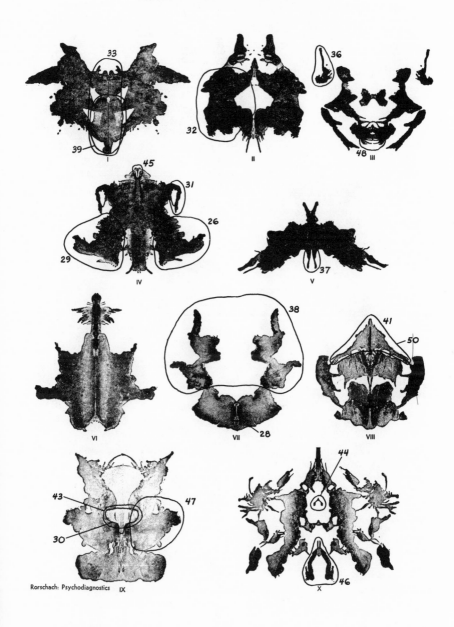

Rorschach: Psychodiagnostics

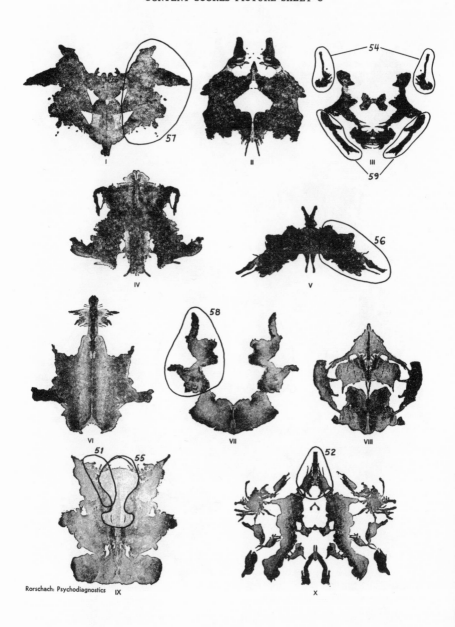

Rorschach: Psychodiagnostics

Ex. No.	Card No.		Loc.	Det.	Con.	P-O

Consult Content Scores Picture Sheet A

1	IV	∨ Head of animal, dragon or something, a strange dragon with a crown.				
		Dragon with eyes, eyelashes, ears, whiskers, nostrils, snout, crowned king.	___	___	___	___
2	VII	Scotty dogs sniffing head of larger dog, noses touching [whole].				
		Looks like Scotty, square face, short tail, and legs.	___	___	___	___
3	VI	A field that's been plowed, furrowed field [whole].				
		A plough went along there and turned the earth over.	___	___	___	___
4	I	Pelvis [whole].				
		Flat smooth spread out surfaces seems skeletal.	___	___	___	___
5	IV	Two dogs sitting down.				
		Dogs just sitting there.	___	___	___	___
6	VIII	A sweetpea.				
		Color and shape of petals.	___	___	___	___
7	VIII	Head of a lamb.	___	___	___	___
8	IX	Witches engaged in some kind of potent activity.				
		Pointed hats, noses, arms, engaged in complex activities of witchcraft. Breasts too big for witches.	___	___	___	___
9	VIII	Might be kind of ice, like Arctic scene—sheet of ice that is blue or and green in color.	___	___	___	___

Ex. No.	Card No.		Loc.	Det.	Con.	P-O
10	VI	Spinal column dissected and opened up.				
		Spinal cord dissected, thin line is nervous tissue.	___	___	___	___
11	X	Gnomes, imaginary figures.				
		Nose, forehead, cap—just top part of body.	___	___	___	___
12	IX	< Viola—with something on the wood —like cello.	___	___	___	___
13	VII	Statues of 2 Greek nymphs.				
		Round cheeks, hair up, stone statue, smooth marble.	___	___	___	___
14	VIII	Head of two bears here looking up.				
		Just see heads, they are looking up.	___	___	___	___
15	VIII	Map of countries with interconnecting waterways [whole, space].				
		The colors show the different countries, these are the waterways. I don't know which countries these could be.	___	___	___	___
16	II	Horseshoe crab.				
		Mostly the shape.	___	___	___	___
17	X	A topographical map.				
		Shading is mountain area, lightest parts are flat lands. Maybe section of some country.	___	___	___	___
18	X	This looks like a horse's head with angry expression in eyes but body form incongruous.				
		Eye here. He looks severe.	___	___	___	___

Ex. No.	Card No.		Loc.	Det.	Con.	P-O

19	X	Leprechauns looking at each other with certain amount of malice but ectoplasm between them so they are related even if they don't like each other.				
		Large foreheads, snub noses, chins, body not well formed. Filmy ectoplasm between them—mad at each other but highly interrelated.	___	___	___	___
20	VIII	This again—kind of a cross-section of human when you take skin off and have muscles on each side and muscles above stomach (stomach is the pink), ribs and on into the neck of the person [whole].				
		Like picture in an anatomy book, colors too.	___	___	___	___
21	I	A penis.				
		Whole central area—no, maybe just this.	___	___	___	___
22	II	Vise holds tools, holds things together.				
		Sections of vise that grasp things.	___	___	___	___
23	X	Tooth in center.				
		I've had two teeth pulled recently.	___	___	___	___
24	VII	Something vaginal about center portion here.				
		Vaginal opening with surrounding dark area, looks like soft hair.	___	___	___	___
25	X	These two might be pink dwarfs, no—babies facing each other.				
		Congenial faces, babies with noses, too smart for babies, pulling against each other, both males. Babies or dwarfs, anyway pink.	___	___	___	___

Ex. No.	Card No.		Loc.	Det.	Con.	P-O

Consult Content Scores Picture Sheet B

26	IV	Seven league boots.				
		Old-fashioned boots.	—	—	—	—
27	VI	Skin of a creature that's been nailed up on a wall, like skin of a racoon, fur markings and striped fur [whole].				
		Head on top.	—	—	—	—
28	VII	Penguin or seal, black.				
		Penguin, white belly, feet.	—	—	—	—
29	IV	Foot upraised.				
		A dance movement.	—	—	—	—
30	IX	Up further the skull of a cow, or deer, horns, nostrils at bottom, two sets of nostrils really.	—	—	—	—
31	IV	Head and neck of swan.				
		They are very graceful.	—	—	—	—
32	II	Gizzard, laminations.				
		General shape and shading.	—	—	—	—
33	I	This is a woman standing with hands raised and feet together.				
		Seen from the back, can't see her head, hands up.	—	—	—	—
34	IV	Whole thing looks like an aviator, sitting on a stool, maybe awaiting orders [whole].				
		Helmet on, sitting back on stool waiting.	—	—	—	—

Ex. No.	Card No.		Loc.	Det.	Con.	P-O
35	II	Clowns playing pattycake, hands come together [whole].				
		Pointed hats, faces, noses, knees together, hands together, color gives it gay feeling. Not actually red faces but color makes it gay.	___	___	___	___
36	III	Girl on a trapeze.				
		Girl hanging on a trapeze, leg outstretched up along rope.	___	___	___	___
37	V	Legs of ballet dancer on her toes, tights on.	___	___	___	___
38	VII	These look like dinosaurs.				
		Tail—head—I saw pictures—This could be dinosaur too—but this part is realistic [S. confused].	___	___	___	___
39	I	A bell.				
		Shape with pendulum sticking out.	___	___	___	___
40	I	∨ Urn old-fashioned, iron arms [whole].				
		Shape of urn, grey of wrought iron.	___	___	___	___
41	VIII	Looks like a snowy mountain.				
		The shape is like a mountain and the greyness is like a snowcap seen from a great distance. The color is sort of shaded in some way.	___	___	___	___
42	IV	An animal pelt [whole].				
		Stretched out to dry, soft fur of animal drying unevenly.	___	___	___	___
43	IX	Some sort of sun dial in a garden.				
		Shape, coloring, white and grey stone.	___	___	___	___

Ex. No.	Card No.		Loc.	Det.	Con.	P-O
44	X	Three balls of pawnbroker.				
		Color.	___	___	___	___
45	IV	Female genitals, I guess.				
		Shading here adds to it I suppose.	___	___	___	___
46	X	Green worms with high aspirations considering idealistic matters.				
		Looking high up and reading.	___	___	___	___
47	IX	< Could be a woman washing clothes.				
		Quite fat.	___	___	___	___
48	III	Pelvic bone.				
		Center again, lower part triangular in shape.	___	___	___	___
49	I	Looks like the bone from an animal [whole, space].				
		Like a bone you would see in a desert. Like a skeleton.	___	___	___	___
50	VIII	This top portion looks like Fuji-yama—distinct peak.				
		The shape looks like it. Looks like a picture taken right there.	___	___	___	___

Consult Content Scores Picture Sheet C

Ex. No.	Card No.		Loc.	Det.	Con.	P-O
51	IX	Looks like reefs—coral reefs.				
		Outline and color—I think coral reefs are very narrow.	___	___	___	___
52	X	Two frogs engaged in a rather profound discussion on the structure of the nervous system of which they have diagram right behind them.				
		On hind legs pointing to diagram of nervous system.	___	___	___	___

Ex. No.	Card No.		Loc.	Det.	Con.	P-O
53	I	Pair of butterflies [whole].				
		Two sides and in middle a cocoon— butterflies coming out of cocoon.	___	___	___	___
54	III	Two little puppets on strings.				
		String, tongue sticking out already, feet suspended from string, not real human quality.	___	___	___	___
55	IX	An hourglass—not a good one— distort time because not same size on top and bottom.	___	___	___	___
56	V	Woman lying down with arms crossed.				
		See head, elbow of crossed arm, and leg. Maybe reclining on a hillside.	___	___	___	___
57	I	< Some kind of mythical animal with animal shape and wings.				
		Head down, maybe grazing, head, wings, haunches of some kind of bull.	___	___	___	___
58	VII	A toy animal.				
		A soft, fluffy stuffed bunny.	___	___	___	___
59	III	∨ A pair of gloves.				
		Long black evening gloves.	___	___	___	___
60	IV	A leafy tree [whole].				
		Shading looks like thick leafy tree— a good shade tree.	___	___	___	___

D. Scoring Categories for the Frequency of the Response

    1. General Definition and Meaning of the Popular and Original Scores

        The popular and original scores are used to denote the frequency with which certain responses are given for specific areas in the blot material. The frequency of a popular response has not been definitely determined. Some experts maintain that a response is "popular" on the basis of a frequency of occurrence of once in every three records. Original responses are based on a frequency of occurrence of once in every hundred records. Most responses are not scored for popularity or originality since they fall between the two extremes of frequency.

       a. The Popular Score

          (1) Popular (P) implies a particular response frequently given to the particular blot area. The ten responses to be scored P are those employed by Klopfer[7] and are presented below:

Card I	(to whole area) Any winged creature with body in center and wings at the sides, seen in action or stationary.
Scoring:	W or W͑ F or FM A P
Card II	(to black area) Any whole animal or part of an animal. The animal should be of the type with a large head and thick neck. Often the texture quality of the skin is used.
Scoring:	W͑ or D FM or Fc A or Ad P
Card III	(to black area) Two human beings, or animals dressed as humans, with legs seen in side bottom areas. The figures must be seen in action.
Scoring:	W or W͑ M H or (A) P
Card III	(center red area) Bow tie or hair ribbon or butterfly. The color may or may not be used.
Scoring:	D F or FC Obj or A P

[7]Because popular responses are statistically determined, they vary among different populations according to age, educational level, cultural setting, and the like. Current happenings may also influence popular responses. For a summary review of popular responses see Levitt and Truumaa (1972, pp. 85–93).

Card IV   None

Card V   (to whole area ∧ or ∨) Any winged creatur⸱ with body in center and wings at the sides. It may be seen in action or stationary.

Scoring: W or Ŵ F or FM A P

Card VI   (to entire card with or without top extension or to entire lower half) Skin of an animal which uses the shading qualities of the blot.

Scoring: W or Ŵ or D Fc Aobj P

Card VII   None

Card VIII   (to outer red area) Almost any four-legged animal given to the pink side area. The animal must be seen in action.

Scoring: D FM A P

Card IX   None

Card X   (to outer blue area) A many-legged animal to the outer blue areas.

Scoring: D F A P

Card X   (to center D in lower green area) Any animal head that has long ears or horns to the light green area between the dark green areas at bottom. If dark green areas are also used, the response should be scored with an additional original.

Scoring: D F Ad P or P + O

Card X   (to lower center D in green area) Any elongated greenish animal to the dark green areas at bottom without the light areas between the darker areas.

Scoring: D FC A P

b. The Original Score

     (1) Original (O) implies the perception of a rarely seen response which is good with respect to form and concept.

         Card VI ∨ These look like dumpy figures of clowns because of baggy clothes, standing with arms around each other, jumping or skipping, some action, one arm outstretched (W). Both on pogo stick.

         Card VII ∨ Looks like prehistoric cave and head of a mammoth carved on each side (W).

    Card VIII   A man going belly-wopping (dd).

    Card V   Also looks like satyrs, half-horse, half-woman, looks as if they are in deep conversation embracing each other, top of them seems to be dressed nicely (W). Horse's hoof here.

    Card VIII   A walking stick, or umbrella with this kind of handle (dr).

    Card IX ∨ Reminds me of cows, bodies of cows as they are being herded through something (D5).
    Cattle, a little fat, see backs, could also be standing and grazing, all looks indefinite.

(2) Bizarre or Inaccurate Original (0—) implies the perception of a rarely seen response which is poor in form and inadequate in concept.

    Card II   Human figure in shorts and shoes (W).
    A fat woman bulging in red and black lacy material, red stockings, leg bent as though dancing on tiptoes (Q) her head could be here.

    Card III   Caterpillar climbing up a string (D2).

    Card IV   Really looks like ghosts because masses are not distinct, two ghosts standing around a tree (dr).
    Looks like they are shooting out pseudopods.

    Card VI   Animal with feet sticking out, shoulders, arms split down the middle (W).
    Buttocks split open.

    Card IX   Face of a man spitting out smoke or something horrible (D7 and D5).
    Eyes here, hissing and emitting stream of fumes.

    Card VI   A caterpillar with butterfly wings stuck on caterpillar's head (dr).

Exercises for the scoring of P-O responses have been omitted since the list of popular responses has been given and the recognition of original responses is a matter of experience. The student should gain some familiarity with original responses as they occur in the scoring exercises and are indicated in the keys.

E. Responses Requiring Multiple Determinant Scores

Some responses require more than one determinant score (or location, or content, or P-O scores) either because they are extensively elaborated during the performance proper or because new information was obtained during the inquiry.

The self-scoring exercises which follow give practice with such responses for the determinant category only.

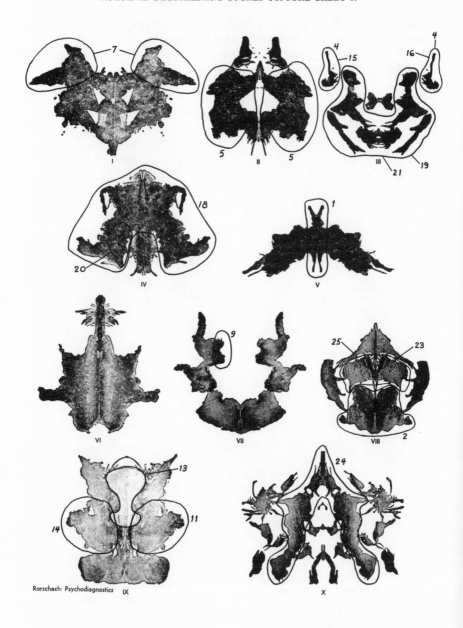

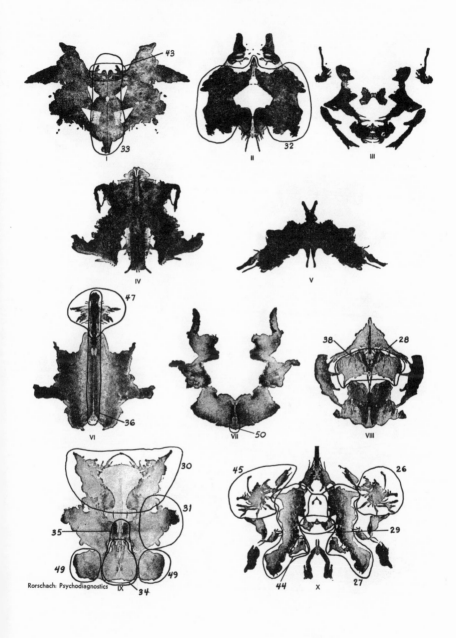

Rorschach: Psychodiagnostics

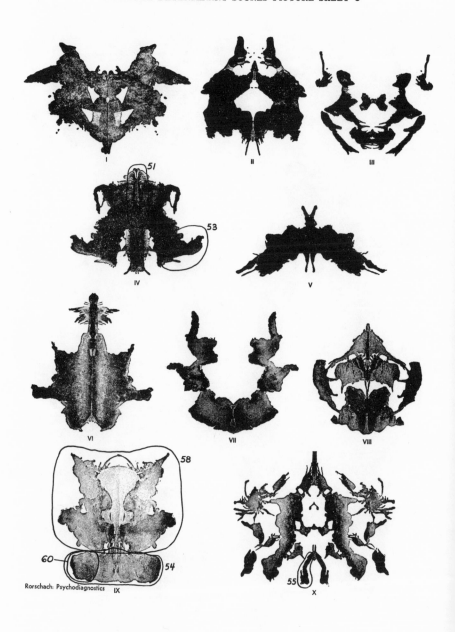

Rorschach: Psychodiagnostics

Ex. No.	Card No.		Loc.	Det.	Con.	P-O

Consult Multiple Determinant Scores Picture Sheet A

1	V	Knock-kneed kid standing here holding up a furry set of wings.				
		Holding up a lot of junk in either hand not wings, like an old hide of some sort.	___	___	___	___
2	VIII	This stuff reminds me of pictures of Grand Canyon, colored pictures with canyon going down.				
		My mother had some, we used to look at years ago.	___	___	___	___
3	IV	Bronte sisters, Wuthering Heights and Jane Eyre [whole].				
		Dark, cloudlike, lot of black, dark moors, weird blowing, thunder and lightning, weird, eery sounds, element of suspense.	___	___	___	___
4	III	Two witches smoking cigars.				
		Got long hat, broomstick, two hands look like end of dust mop, like made of soft material, she is sitting on it and wind is blowing her along.	___	___	___	___
5	II	Double bear.				
		Kinky black bear with no head, shaggy bear.	___	___	___	___
6	II	Looks like a wall that has been shot with a cannon and red-like blood from people who got killed. A hole through the wall [whole, space].				
		Wall is all black part.	___	___	___	___
7	I	Wolves looking off in different directions.				
		Sly wolves looking, the dark-light is not unpleasant, like fur.	___	___	___	___

Ex. No.	Card No.		Loc.	Det.	Con.	P-O
8	VII	>Looks like clouds floating along [whole].	——	——	——	——
9	VII	>Big angry waves with foam on top, large waves ready to splash.	——	——	——	——
10	II	Looks like two witches dancing, they got hands and legs up like that, got hats on, got black coats [whole]. Pointed orange hats.	——	——	——	——
11	IX	Soft green gelatinous mass. Could be jello.	——	——	——	——
12	IX	Pair of dragons insulting each other [whole]. Orange and green is dragon, standing on red, and here is a partition. Smoke coming out of nostril and mouth open and big arm is going to slap each other.	——	——	——	——
13	IX	Looks like a fountain in the back. Keeps getting lighter, squirting water.	——	——	——	——
14	IX	This green blue grass is pretty, picture of mountains far off, color is like Adirondacks.	——	——	——	——
15	III	The two red splashes, looks like lightning flashes illuminating the sky.	——	——	——	——
16	III	Blood dripping down. *CF mↃ* Color splash, streaming down.	——	——	——	——

Ex. No.	Card No.		Loc.	Det.	Con.	P-O

17   VII   Four large rough rocks piled on top of each other in a special way, like scenic rocks for decorative purposes or it could be a natural formation [whole].

The gray color of the rocks and the shading.   ___   ___   ___   ___

18   IV   God, looks like an ape, a raging ape.

He's pounding, grizzly head, this part does not come in.   ___   ___   ___   ___

19   III   Two men in tail coats, white collars bending over a table.

Waiters in uniform pulling a table.   ___   ___   ___   ___

20   IV   Seal climbing down a tree side ways.

I'm not so sure it's a seal because there's a paw, looks like it's black and slippery.   ___   ___   ___   ___

21   III   V   Two old colored men with backs toward each other with hands up in air.

Like a ritual, the way they hold hands up, hair is fuzzy and dark, have whitish whiskers and thick lips. Shading makes it look fuzzy.   ___   ___   ___   ___

22   IV   <   Masses of storm clouds [whole].

I see that all the time, the shading and color.   ___   ___   ___   ___

23   VIII   A blue mist in middle with dim forms in it.

Mists are grayish blue. Forms look like slopes.   ___   ___   ___   ___

Ex. No.	Card No.		Loc.	Det.	Con.	P-O

24   X   Eiffel tower seen across a vista of gardens leading to it.

In distance and beyond is pink flower bed.   ___   ___   ___   ___

25   VIII   Torn pieces of material, silk, the color and form, couldn't be velvet because not heavy enough texture.   ___   ___   ___   ___

<u>Consult Multiple Determinant Scores Picture Sheet B</u>

26   X   Two crabs on either side.

Have a green claw sticking out from arm, I've seen crabs with green claws.   ___   ___   ___   ___

27   X   Two figures wearing parasols, promenading, swaying, carrying kerchiefs like mid-Victorian, maybe they are posing, because of unnatural stance, long gowns with ruffling up the back.

Chiffon handkerchief here, gowned and gloved in same color.   ___   ___   ___   ___

28   VIII   Those look like soft pillows in a feminine house, like in bedroom of Louis XV.

Blue my favorite color, looks soft, satiny and luxurious.   ___   ___   ___   ___

29   X   Like two birds, blue birds, I suppose.

Wings go out like it's flying.   ___   ___   ___   ___

30   IX   Two devils.

Hands outstretched, tall hats, color of devils.   ___   ___   ___   ___

31   IX   Two boys or young tough men with pug noses, wild green hair, probably Irish.   ___   ___   ___   ___

Ex. No.	Card No.		Loc.	Det.	Con.	P-O
32	II	Two little bears with noses to- gether.				
		Little paws, noses up, texture of fur.	___	___	___	___
33	I	In middle is a woman holding her hands over her head, sort of a grotesque type, like a Balinese dancer.				
		Barefooted, legs and hips, head seems divided in two parts, hands in mittens, see legs through dress, transparent dress.	___	___	___	___
34	IX	The lungs of a chicken down in here like when you dissect a chicken.				
		Looks more porous than the heart, the color too, the pocket-like shape.	___	___	___	___
35	IX	Something erupting, fire erupting.	___	___	___	___
36	VI	∨ Paved road with two lanes, dark macadam road.				
		White lines divide two lanes; in perspective.	___	___	___	___
37	IX	Canyon, green plants, water- fall and foam through here, not much life in it, just steady, [whole].				
		When it hits it gives up a cloud of foam and sunshine might give it the reddish color, background here seems way in the distance.	___	___	___	___
38	VIII	I see flags, two flags, they are green and waving.	___	___	___	___

Ex. No.	Card No.		Loc.	Det.	Con.	P-O

39   VII   ∨ Dancing girls, bustles, heads back, Siamese twins, heads not clear, Russian dancers in boots, fur pieces on head, breast, pert noses [whole].

Boots, skirt is tight-waisted, breast, neck, Great Russian fur hats, texture of grey white fur.   ___ ___ ___ ___

40   VII   Looks like a series of masks rising from smoke, two women, dwarfs or goblins and smoke [whole].

Smoke comes up, women have feathers, smoke looks fluffy.   ___ ___ ___ ___

41   I   Like a picture of a storm, black and gray, coming there in waves, storm over the sea [whole].

Light and dark rain clouds.   ___ ___ ___ ___

42   I   Could be a bat or a bird [whole, space].

Head and tail. It's flat on some white surface.   ___ ___ ___ ___

43   I   ∨ Looks like clouds.

Dark grey clouds, just the mass.   ___ ___ ___ ___

44   X   Two men dancing a Spanish dance.

Two men in fluffy shiny Spanish costume, it looks like a Spanish dance because of the way they look.   ___ ___ ___ ___

45   X   Two blue crabs eating green seaweed [side blue and top green].

Not necessarily blue crabs, seaweed green.   ___ ___ ___ ___

46   V   ∧ Lady at a costume ball as some insect [whole].

Burdened, a Carmen Miranda sort of thing, velvety fluff, arms out.   ___ ___ ___ ___

Ex. No.	Card No.		Loc.	Det.	Con.	P-O
47	VI	Looks like a lamppost or a light.				
		Light rays are here.	___	___	___	___
48	VI	< Looks like a fire or explosion in a city by the water and reflection in water, lot of smoke and fire [whole].				
		See the building, explosion shaded that way, light and dark.	___	___	___	___
49	IX	Balloon, shiny round object.				
		The color and the shape.	___	___	___	___
50	VII	Waterfall coming over the mountain.				
		From the distance you see the splashes.	___	___	___	___

Consult Multiple Determinant Scores Picture Sheet C

Ex. No.	Card No.		Loc.	Det.	Con.	P-O
51	IV	Man in dark suit with white shirt, standing with hands in his pocket,· indefinite head, shirt is white and comes down to point where coat is open. Tie is lopsided.				
		Now this man has hands over his head, sort of like a strong man, muscles bulging.	___	___	___	___
52	IV	Reflection of whole thing in water [whole].				
		Beautiful, it's nothing, just a reflection, at least three miles away, see evergreen trees and looks like smoke aurora around fire, heavy black smoke, forest back here.	___	___	___	___
53	IV	Dog sitting down.				
		Wire-haired fox terrier, the head is here, the shape and little furry around nose.	___	___	___	___

Ex. No.	Card No.		Loc.	Det.	Con.	P-O

| 54 | IX | This might be a piece of sea foam washed up on the beach. | | | | |
| | | After a storm, all puffed up and you can crack them, not the exact color, but it's light and cool-looking. | ___ | ___ | ___ | ___ |

| 55 | X | Sky writing, smoky effect, goes up and down again. | ___ | ___ | ___ | ___ |

| 56 | IX < | Looks like a forest scene reflected in water in autumn [whole]. | | | | |
| | | Tree [green], tints of yellow, these leaves about to fall off because they are different colors, not green, you can see the way it looks in the water here. | ___ | ___ | ___ | ___ |

| 57 | IX ∨ | Looks like a clown with pretty flattened-out head, somebody hit him [whole]. | | | | |
| | | Has green coat and orange pants on, he's standing. | ___ | ___ | ___ | ___ |

| 58 | IX | Couple of lobsters in some sea grass. | | | | |
| | | The red colors made me think of lobsters, long feelers, sea grass is green with holes in it. | ___ | ___ | ___ | ___ |

| 59 | I | Like a shield. | | | | |
| | | Four white spots are just decoration on the shield. | ___ | ___ | ___ | ___ |

| 60 | IX > | God of Wind like you see in children's books, you see the weird pictures, big blustery thing. | | | | |
| | | The coloring too is blustery, how the wind is represented. | ___ | ___ | ___ | ___ |

Chapter III

The Technique of Tabulation

The Purpose of Tabulation

The technique of tabulation involves the summarizing of the scoring symbols to facilitate the analysis of the record as a whole. The tabulation includes a listing and summation of all scores, a graphic statement of the proportion among the location, determinant, content, and the popular-original scores, and the calculation of significant percentages and ratios. Reaction time and response time are also recorded.

All workers recognize the value of summarizing the scores. The particular approach adopted, however, varies according to individual needs. A detailed procedure is outlined here which should be especially useful for the beginning student. As he progresses in his Rorschach work, the student may desire to omit some of the steps or perhaps to add some of his own. A comprehensive blank for recording and summarizing a Rorschach protocol is available.[1]

A. How to List and Sum Scores

A separate scoring list is desirable even if the student scores a record in the process of administration. A separate list which clearly includes the main and additional scores in exact order provides a picture of the subject's reaction to each card and to the Rorschach record as a whole. The list also makes the summation for each scoring category easier and thus greater accuracy is assured. For ease in listing scores it is suggested that columns be used as in the example below. In Column 1 is recorded the number of the card, using Roman numerals, and the number of the response, using Arabic numerals; Column 2 may be used to record the reaction time, the total time to each card, and the position of the card when not in the upright position. The next four columns, Nos. 3, 4, 5 and 6, are used for the location, determinant, content, and P-O scores, respectively, subdivided into main and additional columns. It is suggested that all additional scores be listed vertically for accuracy in totaling.

---

[1]B. Klopfer and H. Davidson, Individual Record Blank for the Rorschach Method of Personality Diagnosis. New York: Harcourt Brace Jovanovich, 1962.

Example

1	2	3		4		5		6	
Card Number and Number of Response	Time and Position	Location		Determi- nant		Content		P-O	
		Main	Add	Main	Add	Main	Add	Main	Add
I 1.	4"	W		F		A		P	
2.	∨	D	S	M	FC'	H			
	1' 30"				Fc				

It is now possible to obtain subtotals for all the location scores, for all the determinant scores, for all the content scores, and the number of P and O scores. These totals are needed for drawing a psychograph for the determinant scores and for calculating percentages and ratios. Main and additional scores are always totaled separately. If the main scores are accurately totaled, there will be an equal number of main location, main determinant and main content scores. The total for each of these must equal the total number of main responses (R). The P-O scores do not tally with the other scores because they are not given to every response. The additional scores are not used in any calculations and therefore do not have to be summed. Additional scores, likewise, do not tally among themselves or with the main scores since they are used for describing different conditions. The number of additional scores for any scoring category may be shown, if desired, as: M = 3 + 1; that is, there are three main and one additional M scores.

B. When to Tally Scores

For long records, it may be desirable to tally scores for each of the scoring categories to each card. Tallying makes it possible to find errors quickly because the totals to each card must check for each of the scoring categories. (See Record Blank previously referred to for an illustration of tallying.)

C. The Determinant Categories—The Psychograph

The psychograph is a device recommended for portraying the important quantitative (and also some qualitative) relationships among the determinant scoring categories. On the horizontal axis (see illustration below) may be indicated the major determinant categories; on the vertical axis spaces are provided for indicating the number of each score. A solid bar line is then drawn to show the number of main responses for each determinant, and a dotted line bar, extended upward, is drawn to show the number of additional scores in that category. If desired, the content of the response or the form level (+ or −) may be written in the space thus provided. The student is, of course, free to experiment with any number of possibilities which will help to give him a clear picture of the personality.

The student should observe that in drawing the graph, some of the scores are grouped together for the purpose of giving a clearer picture and also because there are usually few responses in these categories. These scores are:

Fm, mf, m	under $\underline{m}$
Fk, kF, k	under $\overline{k}$
KF, K	under $\overline{K}$
cF, c	under $\overline{c}$
FC', C'F, C'	under $\overline{C}$'
C, Cdes, Cn, Csym	under $\overline{C}$

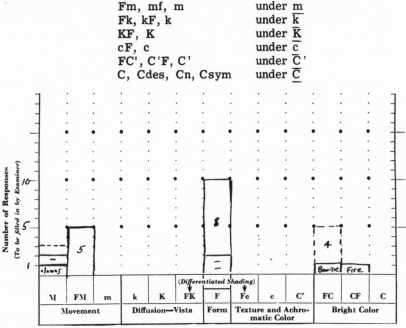

Determinant Categories

D. The Location Categories—Table of Percentages

The relation of each category of location score (W, D, d, Dd and/or S) to the total number of responses is calculated in percentages. (Example: R = 30; W = 8; W% = 8/30 or 27%). These percentages are used to analyze the relationship among the scoring categories, that is, W% to D%, D% to d% and so forth, as well as to determine how close the obtained percentage is to the expected percentage for that score.

A table of expected percentages for each location scoring category is given below for handy reference.

Several degrees of underemphasis, indicated by single and double parentheses, and several degrees of overemphasis, indicated by underlinings, of each of the location categories are shown. These degrees of over- and underemphasis are based on a study of the statistical frequency with which the scores appear. The normal expectancy is shown within the two solid lines, that is, a majority of people give 20-30% W's, 45-55% D's; 5-15% d's and less than 10% Dd plus S scores.

W	D	d	Dd $\frac{\text{and}}{\text{or}}$ S
< 10% ((W)) 10-20 (W) 20-30 W 30-45 W̲ 45-60 W̳ >60 W̳	< 30% ((D)) 30-45 (D) 45-55 (D 55-65 D̲ 65-80 D̳ > 80 D̳	< 5% (d) 5-15 d 15-25 d̲ 25-35 d̳ 35-45 d̳ >45 d̳	< 10% Dd S 10-15 Dd S̲ 15-20 Dd S̳ 20-25 Dd S̳ > 25 Dd S̳

E. Recording of Other Factors

Other quantitative factors, such as the number of responses (R), the reaction time, the response time, etc., required for interpretation, should be noted. Always show the number of main responses first, followed, if desired, by the number of additional responses thus: Total Responses (R) = 20 + 5. All time factors relate to time during the performance proper since time during the inquiry is not noted at all.

1. Percentages

A number of scores are translated into percentages since the interpretation of their significance is in part a function of their relation to the total number of responses. Only main responses are used to calculate percentages. The percentages most frequently computed are:

$$F\% = \frac{\text{Total F}}{R} \qquad A\% = \frac{A + Ad}{R}$$

$$\frac{FK + F + Fc}{R} = \quad \% \qquad \frac{\text{No. R VIII} + IX + X}{R} = \quad \%$$

2. Ratios[2]

The relationship between certain scores are important for interpretation. These ratios are recorded for the main responses only. The important ratios are:

$$\text{sum C} = \frac{FC + 2CF + 3C}{2} \qquad \text{M:sum C} = \quad :$$

$$(FM + M):(Fc + c + C') = \quad : \qquad W:M = \quad :$$

---

[2] Other ratios, like M: FM, FC:(CF + C) are considered by Klopfer and Davidson (1954, p. 125). In these ratios, additional scores are included, giving them a weighting of one-half.

3. Succession[3]

Succession refers to the order in which the location categories are used. When the individual responds to all 10 cards systematically (e.g., W, D, d; D, d, or S, or the reverse) then this pattern is defined as rigid; if the pattern occurs in 7-9 cards it is considered orderly; loose in 3-6 cards; and confused in less than 3 cards.

4. Estimate of Intellectual Level

An estimate of intellectual capacity and efficiency may be made from a careful consideration of the following factors:

number and quality of W	level of form accuracy
number and quality of M	variety of content
number and quality of O	succession

5. Location Charts

Location charts are needed by the examiner to outline the area used for each response, especially for locations that are unusual. These outlines should be carefully executed and accurately numbered to correspond to the number of the response.

---

[3]For further details on succession, see Klopfer et al. (1954, pp. 314-315).

Chapter IV

Technique of Administration

A. General Considerations

    1. Testing Atmosphere

        The atmosphere in which the Rorschach test is adminis-
tered should be as relaxed as the circumstances allow. The
child, especially the young child, should have an opportunity
to become familiar with the surroundings and may have to
move about from time to time during the testing.

        An explanation of how the blots were made may be indi-
cated and will be dependent upon such factors as the age of
the subject, his cultural background and sophistication with
respect to test situations. The subject is encouraged to respond freely. With the exception of these one or two state-
ments by way of introducing the subject to the test, there
are as few comments as possible in order that the subject's
response to the blot material may be spontaneous.

    2. Seating Arrangement

        The examiner as well as the subject should be able to
see the cards easily during the administration of the test. A
recommended arrangement is that the examiner sit to the
side and slightly back of the subject. An arrangement
whereby the subject sits beside the examiner, or examiner
sits facing the subject, may be preferred. When working
with young children it is most helpful to sit side by side.

    3. Essential Materials

        The ten Rorschach cards

        Location chart (a sheet on which is reproduced the ten
ink blots for use in marking out location areas)

        Pen or pencil, paper

        Noiseless stop watch or regular watch with second hand

B. The Testing Procedure

    The administration of the Rorschach test may be divided into
two main phases: 1. The Performance Proper; 2. The Inquiry.

    1. The Performance Proper

        The Performance Proper consists of the subject's re-
sponses to the initial presentation of the cards.

        a. Instructions to Subject

            The Rorschach test has no standard directions for
the subject. A number of formulations have been suggested. One example of an acceptable formulation is
as follows:

"People see all sorts of things in these
ink blot pictures; now tell me what you
see, what it might be for you, what it
makes you think of."

The subject may ask questions such as whether
turning the card is permissible or whether he may give
more than one response. Such questions should be an-
swered in a general way by a statement such as, "That
is entirely up to you." If necessary, continue by saying,
"There are no right or wrong answers. People see all
sorts of different things in these blots."

b. Presentation of Cards
The ten cards are presented one at a time in upright position from the stack placed face down on the
table with Card I on top and Card X at the bottom. The
cards must be presented in sequence, starting with
Card I and ending with Card X.

It is advisable to ask the subject to hold the card
when it is presented to him and to indicate that he is to
continue holding it until he is through responding. The
subject is further instructed to put the card face down
on the table when he has finished. The subject thus
indicates that he is ready to proceed with the next card.

c. Recording of Responses
It is suggested that the paper which is used for
recording be divided in half lengthwise. The column on
the left may then be used for recording verbatim the
responses obtained during the performance proper; the
column on the right may then be used to record information obtained during the inquiry. Usually recording the
inquiry requires more space than the data of the performance proper. New responses may also be added
during the inquiry. It is therefore advisable to leave
plenty of space between each response, thus enabling
the examiner to record the inquiry data alongside the
appropriate responses given in the performance proper.

All verbalizations, remarks, as well as responses
should be recorded.

d. Numbering the Responses
Number with arabic numbers the responses given
to each card. Begin each card with number 1. Some
workers number the responses in continuous sequence
throughout the ten cards. The former method is preferred because totals for each card as well as the total
responses for all ten cards are readily obtained. Sometimes it is not possible to determine whether the subject

has given one response or merely a remark not to be considered a response. In such instances, numbering should be delayed until the inquiry, at which time the specific information can be elicited.

e. Recording of Time

Two time notations are usually made: (1) reaction time and (2) response time.

(1) Reaction time is the time between the presentation of the card and the subject's first response to it. A silent stop watch, or a standard watch with a second hand, may be used. Reaction time is recorded in ten instances, once for each card. Intervals between responses to the same card may also be noted if they seem to be significantly long.

(2) Response time is the length of time taken to complete the performance proper. Some workers note the time required for each card; others merely note the time when the test is begun and again when the performance proper is over. Total time is then divided by the total number of responses, which gives the average time per response.

f. Recording of Position of Card

No notation is made when responses are given to the card in the upright position, that is, when the card is not turned. The symbols used to note the positions are:

$<$ indicates top of card is to the left

$>$ indicates top of card is to the right

$\vee$ indicates top of card is at the bottom

⊚   indicates that the card has been turned several times

$\wedge$ indicates that the card has been turned so that the top is again in the upright position

2. The Inquiry

a. Purpose

An inquiry, following the performance proper, is conducted to obtain sufficient information so that a response can be scored correctly. An inquiry is necessary only for those responses where such information is not implicit or not clearly indicated in the response itself.

The inquiry should determine, when necessary, the three factors of location, determinant and content. In other words, the examiner must ascertain exactly what part of the blot was used for the concept, what determinant or determinants were used, and exactly what content was seen.

The inquiry can be conducted in the usual way when testing most children. Modification in the inquiry procedure may be called for in the case of the exceptional child; for example, with the hyperactive child the inquiry can follow each response.

b. Orientation

Two important considerations should be kept in mind in conducting the inquiry.

(1) The subject should not be made to feel that his concepts are being challenged. He should be put at ease by some remark like, "Now you have seen all the cards and given your answers. Let us go over your answers together because I want to be sure that I see them the way you do." If the subject seems to need further assurance, say something like, "Your answers are very interesting and I'd like to know what in the blot suggested them."

(2) The subject should not become aware of the kinds of information the examiner is seeking. Suggestions for eliciting the kinds of information needed are given below.

c. Recording during Inquiry

The record of the inquiry should include both the questions of the examiner and the responses of the subject.

(1) What Examiner Says

When the examiner asks a question beyond the initial one, such questioning should at least be recorded by a notation like (Q) to give an indication of the amount of prodding necessary. If, however, the beginning student wishes to submit his inquiry for later criticism he should, of course, record the complete and exact question or questions asked.

(2) What Subject Says

The subject's elaboration, if any, of the responses given during the performance proper is recorded directly opposite the response to which it refers. Some information like location area or parts of unusual concepts can be recorded directly on the location chart by the examiner.

New responses given during the inquiry should be recorded when they occur and in the order in which they are given (additional responses).

Significant remarks, of course, should also be noted.

d. Inquiry Procedures
   (1) Procedures for Determining Location
      Information regarding location, if the location is unclear, may best be elicited by saying, "Show me where on the blot you saw _____," or merely, "Where is the _____?"

      If this does not result in a clear idea, other methods may be used: (1) the subject may be asked to use his finger or blunt end of pencil to outline the area directly on the blot; (2) the subject may be asked to outline with pencil the area he used for his concept on the location chart; (3) he may be asked to take a sheet of tracing paper and outline the area. Rarely do the latter two methods have to be resorted to.

      When the location area has been determined and if the area used is not a usual one, the examiner should outline it on the location chart. Number the outline to correspond to the number of the response. Sometimes it may be desirable to qualify further the different parts of the concept seen, like the head, or the legs, or the petals, and the like. (See Record No. 1).
   (2) Procedures for Ascertaining Determinants
      Information concerning the determinant or determinants used is somewhat more difficult to obtain. It is advisable that the examiner avoid unnecessary questions as well as direct questions. The possibility of influencing the subject's response is thereby reduced. The kind of questioning to be employed will often depend upon what the subject says and what is implied in his response.

      If the examiner doesn't already know about the determinants used, a good first question is:
      "Describe the . . . . in detail."
               or
      "Tell me how you see . . ."
               or
      "Tell me more about the way you see . . ."
               or
      "What about the blot makes it look like . . ."
      Usually questions such as the aforementioned will yield enough information so that the examiner will be able to score them.
      (a) Form
         If a concept with definite form is given, the quality of the form may be in question.

Queries such as, "Where are the wings?" or "What about the legs?" in instances for example where an insect or some animal is given usually clarify for the examiner how clearly the concept is seen.

(b) Movement

Where it is necessary or advisable to determine whether the human figures seen are in action, one, or at most, two prodding questions such as the following may be asked:

"What about this part? (as center detail in III) Does it belong to the figure you see?"

or

"How do you see the legs or arms?" (in instances where the subject has included legs or arms in his response)

Direct questions, such as "Are they bowing?" or "What are they doing?" should in no instance be asked.

Animal action, when seen at all, is usually clearly so indicated by the subject. Questions similar to those with respect to human figures may be asked when the examiner wishes to determine whether the subject sees the animal in action. (This practice is usually limited to the animals in VIII.)

(c) Color

The use of color must be clearly indicated or implied in the concept seen if it is to be scored. Flowers, landscapes, fire, explosions, etc., seen in colored areas of the cards are usually scored for color without further inquiry unless there is strong indication to the contrary.

Inquiry problems are present mainly in two instances, one with responses which use both color and form and where there is doubt whether the response should be scored FC or CF. In this case the examiner should try to determine the definiteness of the form seen. The following are examples of questions which have been found helpful in eliciting information concerning color and form.

"What kind of flower is it?"

or

"What about the blot makes it look like like an underwater scene?"

Where the subject replies with a definite form concept like "tulip" it is clearly an FC response. If he says, "Oh, it could be any kind of flower," the necessary information has been obtained and the response is scored CF.

The other inquiry problem, concerned with concepts like "butterfly" given to the red areas in either Cards II or III or "tree" to some area in Cards VIII or IX, may or may not involve the use of color. It then becomes necessary to determine whether the concept involves form only or whether color is also used in a clear FC combination. At least one prodding question should be asked, as, "What about this part made it look like a . . .?" or, if necessary, "Was it just the shape that made you think of it?"

(d) Shading

Shading responses often require careful and delicate inquiry since shading is often merely implied in a response and not directly expressed. The examiner should ask at least one prodding question to attempt to determine whether or not shading is used.

Queries such as "What side of the bear skin do you see?"

and then perhaps

"What makes it look like the under (or upper) side (in instances where the response is, "A bear rug")

or

"You said this looks like a totem pole. Is there anything about this part of the blot in addition to the shape that made you think of a totem pole?"

(3) Procedures for Ascertaining Content

Inquiry concerning content is usually unnecessary. There is, however, one exception. When a subject says he sees "figures," the examiner should determine whether they are human or animal, and, if human, whether man or woman. In these instances direct questions may be employed.

e. Final Remarks Concerning the Inquiry

The inquiry will become simple and inappropriate questioning will be reduced if the examiner takes his clues for questioning from what the subject has implied in his response and from the words actually used by him. For example, a response is given like, "This looks like a pretty flower." Immediately the word "pretty" suggests that the subject is emphasizing color in his concept. The examiner should then say, "You said this was a pretty flower, what makes it look pretty?"

Another suggestion to the examiner is to go back to previous responses for analogous situations, such as "In this card you said the shading gave you the idea; is that also true here?"

One additional word of warning to the beginner: it is better to ask too little than to ask too much. Pressing for determinants not actually used by the subject will distort a Rorschach protocol to a greater extent than overlooking one or two determinants.

3. Testing the Limits

The "testing the limits" phase of administration involves the use of special techniques to determine whether or not a subject is capable of seeing specific kinds of responses or of using specific determinants which the subject has not used in his spontaneous reactions. A good deal of experience, especially in interpretation, helps to develop the rationale on which the worker bases his handling of this phase of the administration. Some workers question the use of "testing the limits." One objection given is that it may influence retest results.

The usual procedure with children is to eliminate "testing the limits." The reason is that it may affect future testing and thereby obscure developmental trends.

Chapter V

Scoring and Developmental Trends

A. General Considerations

The Rorscharch reflects developmental changes. It is important in working with the records of adults, as well as with those
of children and adolescents, to be aware of the expected age norms
for the scoring categories. Normative studies of children and
adolescents have been done by Ames (1971, 1974), Hertz (1960),
Ledwith (1960), and Levitt and Truumaa (1972). Norms for adults
have also been reported in the Rorschach literature. These
studies show consistent trends in age norms, although exact
averages may differ from study to study. Insofar as this Workbook is primarily concerned with scoring, we will not attempt a
detailed review of developmental norms. Rather we will illustrate
broad trends and the changes in the major determinants that occur
with age, in order to give the beginning student a feeling of what
to expect. The numerical figures for the various scoring categories
should not be regarded as exact numbers, but as reflecting general
trends. They will be summarized at the end of this chapter.

B. Changes in Major Scoring Categories with Age
    1. Number of Responses
        In general, the number of responses increases from approx-
    imately 10-15 at age five, to about 18 or 19 at ages eight to
    eleven, and from ages twelve to sixteen the number of re-
    sponses increases slowly to about 20. Normal adults are ex-
    pected to give no less than 20 responses and usually between
    20 and 30 responses.
    2. Location Categories
        The W% decreases with increase in age. At age five, W% is
    55-60, decreasing to 50% at age ten, and by fourteen it is down
    to approximately 43%. The W% decreases further during ado-
    lescence and approaches the expected norm of 20-30% for
    adults. The distribution of the D% also fluctuates throughout
    childhood, but in general has been found to vary between
    40-50%, which is also the expected range for normal adults.

3. Form Responses

In considering the F%, it should be clear that the F% decreases as the use of other determinants increases. In general, F% decreases with age, while the F+% increases. At age five, F% is approximately 67%. It decreases to about 60% at age ten and stays at that level through most of adolescence. Normal adults are expected to have an F% of about 50 or less.

4. Movement Responses

The norms for movement responses are concerned not only with the absolute numbers of each kind of movement response, but also with the relation between the kinds of movement determinants in any given record. In particular we are always interested in the relationship between human movement responses (M) and animal movement responses (FM). There is usually one human movement response in the record of a five-year-old. This may double at age seven. From age seven through adolescence the average human movement responses may remain about two. In later adolescence human movement responses approach three, which is the norm for adults. In the early years there are usually more FM than M responses. By adolescence, the numbers may equal each other, and the shift to more M than FM does not occur until late adolescence. For normal adults it is expected that the number of M will be at least 3 and will equal or exceed the number of FM responses.

5. Color Responses

With color responses, as with movement responses, the developmental norms are concerned not only with the individual determinants, but also with the relation between the various color determinants (FC: CF + C) and with the ratio of the sum of all the color responses to human movement responses (M : ΣC). In the records of children and adolescents there may be twice as many CF responses as FC responses. By late adolescence the number of FC responses may be equal to the number of CF + C responses. The normal adult record is expected to have more FC than CF responses. No C responses are expected in the normal adult record. The ratio of M to all color responses shifts at about age ten. Before that age, the sum of the color responses exceeds human movement responses, and then, through adolescence, the ratio reverses. The expected ratio of human movement to color responses in the normal adult record is also (M > ΣC).

6. Shading Responses

Shading responses are rare in children's records, may occur in adolescents' records, and in adult records there may be one or two such responses.

7. Animal and Human Content Responses

Animal responses constitute about 50% through the ages of five to eleven, dropping after that to about 40%. Adult records are not expected to exceed 40%. The percentage of human content responses increases with age. The expectation is about 10% at age five, 15% at age eight, with a slow increase through adolescence, until human content responses approach the average of 20%, which is expected in adult records.

8. Popular and Original Responses

The average five-year-old can be expected to give two popular responses, the eight-year-old, about three populars, and the adolescent, an average of five. Three to five popular responses are the expected norm for adults. There are no norms established for original responses and they may occur at all age levels.

C. Summary

The data presented in the proceeding section are summarized in the chart below.

SUMMARY OF DEVELOPMENTAL TRENDS

SCORING CATEGORIES	Ages			
	5	8 to 11	12 to 16	Adult
R	10–15	18–19	19–20	20–30
W%	58%	50%	43%	20–30%
D%	40–50%	40–50%	40–50%	40–50%
F%	67%	60%	60%	50%
F%	70%	80%	80–90%	90%
M	1	2	2–3	3
FM	2	4	3	2–3
FC	<1	<1	1	2
CF + C	2	2	1	1
FC:CF + C	1:2	1:2	1:1	FC > CF + C
M:ΣC	M < ΣC	M < ΣC	M > ΣC	M > ΣC
A%	50%	40%	40%	40%
H%	10%	15%	18%	20%
P	2	3	3	5

Appendix 1

Keys to Self—Testing Exercises

a. Key to Location Scores

Item No.	Loc.	Det.	Con.	P-O	Item No.	Loc.	Det.	Con.	P-O
1	W	F	A	P	24	D	M	(H)	
2	dd	F	Dust		25	S	F	Ad	
3	W	F	Aobj	P	26	di	FM	Ad	
4	d	F	Ad		27	D	FM	A	
5	D→W	FM	A	P	28	dr	M	H	
6	D, W.	F	(H)		29	d	Fc	Sex	
7	D	FM	A	→P	30	dr	F—	Art	
8	D	F	A	P	31	D	cF	Food	
9	d	M	H		32	D, S	FC'	Ad	
10	D	M	H		33	W, S	F	Mask	
11	D→W	M—	(H)		34	de	F	Hd	
12	W, S	Fm, FK, FC'	Obj	O	35	d	F	Ad	
13	dd	F	Ad		36	D	F	Obj	
14	dr	Fc	Hd		37	d	F	Obj	O
15	D	M	Hd		38	dr, S	F	Obj	O
16	S	F	A		39	dr	FM	Ad	O
17	dr	FC'	N		40	d	F	Obj	
18	dr	F	Hd		41	D	M	Hd	
19	D→W	FM	A	P	42	S	F	Obj	
20	dr	FM	A		43	dr	F	Hd	
21	W⎫ D ⎬W D ⎭	M mF Csym	H Sex Obj	P	44	W	M	H	
					45	d	FM	Ad	
22	di	F	Hd		46	D	F	Obj	O
23	D, S	F	Ad		47	D	F	Geo	

Item No.	Loc.	Det.	Con.	P-O	Item No.	Loc.	Det.	Con.	P-O
48	W	FM	A	P	62	d	F	Ad	
49	dr	F—	A		63	dd	F	At	
50	D,S	F	At		64	dr	M	H	
51	dr	FM	A	O	65	D	M	H	
52	W	F,FM—	A,Pl		66	D	F	Art	
53	d	FM	A		67	W	M,FC'	(H)	
54	W	FM	A	P	68	W	M,CF	(H)	
55	di	F	Ad	O—	69	D⎫ D⎬W D⎭	FC FC FC	Food Food Food	
56	DW	FM—	A						
57	W	M	(H)		70	W	M	H	
58	dd	F	Ad		71	D	Fc	(Ad)	
59	d	F	Ad		72	dd	FC	Food	
60	D	C/F	At		73	d	M	Hd	
61	dr	M	(H)		74	S →W	C'F,F—	Pl	
					75	D	F	(H)	

b. KEY TO FORM SCORES

Item No.	Loc.	Det.	Con.	P-O	Item No.	Loc.	Det.	Con.	P-O
1	W	F	A	P	8	d	F	Obj	
2	D	F	A		9	W,S	F	Ad	
3	WS	F—	H		10	dr	F	Hd	
4	D,S	F	A	O	11	dr	F	At	
5	D	F—	Arch	O—	12	D	F	Hd	
6	D	F	Obj		13	D	F	Pl	
7	D	F	Ad		14	D	F	A	P

Item No.	Loc.	Det.	Con.	P-O	Item No.	Loc.	Det.	Con.	P-O
15	D	F	A		46	d	F	Hd	
16	D	F	Obj	O	47	D	F	Obj	
17	dr	F	A		48	D	F	Aobj	
18	D	F	A	P	49	D	F	A	
19	dr	F	Sex		50	S	F	A	
20	d	F	Sex		51	W	F−	A	
21	d	F	Ad		52	d	F	Ad	
22	dd	F	Hd		53	W	F	A	P
23	D	F	Hd		54	dr,S	F	Geo	
24	W,S	F	Mask		55	D	F−	At	
25	d	F	Pl		56	d	F	Ad	
26	W	F	A	P	57	W	F−	A	
27	d	F+	Hd		58	dd	F	Ad	
28	D	F	A		59	D	F	Obj	
29	W	F	A		60	W	F−	Obj	O−
30	S	F	Obj		61	d	F	A	
31	W	F−	A		62	W	F−	A	
32	D,S	F	At		63	dd	F	Obj	O
33	d	F	N		64	dd	F	Ad	
34	D	F	Ad		65	d	F	Ad	
35	D	F	Ad		66	dd	F	Ad	
36	D	F	N		67	dr	F+	Obj	
37	dr	F	Ad		68	dd	F	Geo	
38	S	F−	At	O−	69	D	F−	Sex	
39	D	F−	A	O−	70	D	F	Geo	
40	dd	F	N		71	S,D	F	Obj	O
41	D	F	Ad	P	72	dd	F	Hd	
42	D	F−	Ad		73	d	F	Ad	
43	d	F	Ad		74	D	F	Aobj	
44	d	F	Obj		75	D	F	Ad	
45	D	F	Obj						

c. KEY TO MOVEMENT SCORES

Item No.	Loc.	Det.	Con.	P-O	Item No.	Loc.	Det.	Con.	P-O
1	D	FM	A		29	D	FM	A	
2	W	FM−	A		30	D	M	Hd	
3	W̄,S	Fm	Hd		31	d	M	Hd	
4	D	Fm	Sex		32	W	FM	A	
5	D	FM	A		33	W	mF	Pl	
6	W	M	H		34	W̄	FM	A	
7	W	M	(H)	O	35	D	M	H	O
8	d	Fm	Pl	O	36	W	mF	Abs	O
9	D	M	H		37	W̄	M	H	P
10	D	FM	A		38	D	M−	H	
11	W̄	M	H		39	W	mF	Obj	O
12	W	FM−	A		40	d	FM	Ad	
13	D	Fm	(H)		41	W̄	M	(A)	P
14	D	M	(A)	O	42	D	Fm	Sex	
15	D	M	(A)		43	W	FM	A	P
16	W̄	M	H		44	D	FM	A	
17	d	M	Hd	O	45	D	m	Abs	O
18	dr,S	Fm	Hd		46	dr	M	H	
19	W	M	H		47	d	FM	A	
20	D	M	H		48	D	FM	A	P
21	d	Fm	Obj		49	W	FM	A	P
22	W	FM	A	P	50	W,S	mF	Explosion	
23	W̄	FM−	A		51	D	FM	A	
24	D	M	H		52	W̄	FM	Ad	
25	W	Fm	Obj		53	D	mF	Abs,Sex	
26	W̄	FM	A		54	W	M	H	
27	W	M	H		55	d	Fm	Pl	
28	dd	F→M	Hd		56	D	M	H	

Item No.	Loc.	Det.	Con.	P-O	Item No.	Loc.	Det.	Con.	P-O
57	dr	M	Hd		67	D	M	(A)	
58	W	mF	Abs	O	68	W	Fm—	Sex	O—
59	D	FM	A		69	W	M	(H)	
60	D	M	(H)		70	D	FM	(A)	
61	D	Fm	(H)		71	D	M	Hd	
62	D	FM	A		72	D	FM	A	
63	W	M	H		73	W	M	H	+O
64	D	FM	A	+O	74	W	FM	A	
65	W	M	H		75	W	M	(H)	
66	d	M	H						

d. KEY TO COLOR SCORES

Item No.	Loc.	Det.	Con.	P-O	Item No.	Loc.	Det.	Con.	P-O
1	D	FC	Obj		16	W	CF	N	
2	W	FC	Pl	O	17	D	FC	Obj	
3	D	FC	A		18	S,W	C'F	N	
4	D	C'F	smoke		19	D,S	CF	N	
5	D	FC'	A		20	D	C'F	Pl	
6	D	FC'	(A)		21	S	C sym	Abs	
7	D	FC—	A		22	S	FC'	Obj	
8	W	C'des	Abs		23	W	CF	Fire	
9	D	CF	Pl		24	D,S	F/C	Sex	
10	d	FC	food		25	W	F/C	At	
11	D	FC'	H		26	W	C'n	Abs	
12	W	Csym	Abs		27	W	F/C	At	
13	W	C/F	At		28	W	FC	Pl	
14	D	CF	Art		29	D	CF	Food	
15	dr	FC	Ad		30	D	FC'	At	O

Item No.	Loc.	Det.	Con.	P-O	Item No.	Loc.	Det.	Con.	P-O
31	D	FC	(A)		54	W,S	Csym	Abs	
32	W	C'F	Art		55	D	CF	Food	
33	W	CF	Art		56	D	FC'	Ad	
34	W	CF	N		57	D	CF	Sex	
35	dd	FC'	Ice		58	D	CF	Art	
36	D	FC	Obj		59	W,S	FC'	A	P
37	W	CF	N		60	W	Cdes	Art	
38	D	FC	(H)	O	61	W	Cn	Colors	
39	W	C'F	Ink		62	D	CF	Fire	
40	W	F/C—	At		63	D	FC	Obj	O
41	dr	FC'	Obj	O	64	D	CF	Obj	
42	W	C/F	At		65	d	FC'	(Hd)	
43	D	C'n	Abs		66	D	FC	Obj	P
44	D	C	N		67	W	Cn	Colors	
45	D	C	N		68	D	FC	At	
46	d	FC'	N		69	D	FC	Ad	O
47	D	C	Bl		70	d	FC'	Arch	
48	D	FC	(Hd)		71	W	FC'sym	Abs	
49	d	FC	Ad		72	W	C'F	Hair	O
50	W	Cdes	Art		73	D	FC	Hd	
51	D	FC	Obj		74	W	Cdes	Abs	
52	D	FC	A		75	D	F/C	Geo	
53	D	FC—	Food						

e. KEY TO SHADING SCORES

Item No.	Loc.	Det.	Con.	P-O	Item No.	Loc.	Det.	Con.	P-O
1	D	Fc	A		29	W	Fk	Map	
2	D	Fk	At		30	D	c	Abs	
3	dr	FK	N		31	D	kF	Map	
4	W	FK	N		32	D,S	F K	N	
5	W	c	Abs		33	dd	FK	Arch	O
6	D	Fc	Obj	O	34	di	Fk	At	
7	dr	kF	Geo		35	W	kF	At	
8	D	cF	N		36	D	Fc	Pl	
9	D,S	kF	Map		37	D	cF	Food	
10	D	Fc	Pl		38	W,S	FK	N	
11	D	Fc	Art		39	D	Fk	At	
12	d	FK	Scene		40	W,S	FK	N	
13	D	Fc	Art		41	D	Fc	Aobj	P
14	D	cF	Obj		42	D	Fk	Arch	O
15	d	Fc	N		43	D	Fk	Map	
16	W,S	FK	N		44	D	FK	N	
17	W,S	FK	Geo		45	W	cF	Abs	
18	D	Fc	A		46	W,S	Fk	At	
19	D	Fc	Obj		47	W	Fc	Obj	
20	S,dr	Fc	N	O	48	D	Fk—	At	
21	D	KF	Clouds (H)		49	W	cF	N	
22	D	Fc	A		50	D	Fk	N	
23	D	cF	Obj	O	51	dr	Fc	Aobj	
24	dr	K	Cloud		52	D	Fc	A	
25	D	FK	N		53	W	FK	N	
26	D	Fc	A		54	W	KF	Smoke	
27	D	cF	Aobj		55	D	Fk	At	
28	W	K	Clouds		56	D	Fc	Art	
					57	W	KF	N	

Item No.	Loc.	Det.	Con.	P-O	Item No.	Loc.	Det.	Con.	P-O
58	W	kF	Obj		67	W	KF	Smoke	
59	D	KF	Cloud		68	d	Fc	Art	
60	D	Fc	A		69	dr	Fc	A	
61	D	cF	Obj		70	D	Fc	Art	
62	D	kF	Geo		71	D	Fc	Obj	
63	W	KF	Smoke		72	D	cF	Obj	
64	D	FK	N		73	dd	cF	Obj	
65	D	Fk	At		74	dd	FK	Arch	O
66	dr,S	K	N		75	D	K	N	

f. KEY TO CONTENT SCORES

Item No.	Loc.	Det.	Con.	P-O	Item No.	Loc.	Det.	Con.	P-O
1	D	F	(Ad)		18	dr	F → M	Ad	
2	W	FM	A		19	D	M,Fc	(H)	+O
3	W	FK	N		20	W	F/C	At	
4	W	Fc	At		21	D	F	Sex	
5	D	FM	A		22	d	F	Obj	
6	D	FC	Pl		23	dd	F	H obj	
7	d	F	Ad		24	d	Fc	Sex	
8	D	M	(H)		25	D	M,FC	(H)	
9	D	CF	N		26	D	F	Obj	
10	D	F	At		27	W	Fc	Aobj	P
11	D	F	(Hd)		28	d	FC'	A	O
12	dr,S	F	Obj		29	D	M	Hd	
13	D	Fc	(Hd)		30	D,S	F	AAt	
14	d	FM	Ad		31	d	F	Ad	
15	W,S	C/F	Geo		32	D	Fc	AAt	O
16	D	F	A		33	D	M	H	
17	D	kF	Geo		34	W	M	H	

Item No.	Loc.	Det.	Con.	P-O	Item No.	Loc.	Det.	Con.	P-O
35	W	M FC$_{sym}$	<u>H</u>		48	D	F	<u>At</u>	
36	D	M	<u>H</u>	O	49	W,S	F	<u>AAt</u>	
37	d	M	<u>Hd</u>		50	D	F	<u>Geo</u>	
38	D	F—	<u>A</u>	O—	51	dr	CF	<u>N</u>	
39	D	F	<u>Obj</u>		52	D	M	<u>(A)</u>	+O
40	W	FC '	<u>Obj</u>		53	W	FM	<u>A</u>	
41	D	FK,FC'	<u>N</u>		54	D	F	<u>(H)</u>	
42	W	Fc	<u>Aobj</u>		55	D,S	F	<u>Obj</u>	
43	D,S	FC'	<u>Obj</u>	O	56	D	M	<u>H</u>	
44	D	FC	<u>Obj</u>		57	D	FM	<u>(A)</u>	O
45	d	Fc	<u>Sex</u>		58	D	Fc	<u>AObj</u>	
46	D	M,FC	<u>(A)</u>	+O	59	D	FC'	<u>Obj</u>	O
47	D	M	<u>H</u>	+O	60	W	Fc	<u>Pl</u>	

g. KEY TO MULTIPLE DETERMINANT SCORES

Item No.	Loc.	Det.	Con.	P-O	Item No.	Loc.	Det.	Con.	P-O
1	D→W	<u>M,Fc</u>	H,Aobj	+O	10	W	<u>M,FC</u> <u>FC'</u>	(H)	
2	D	<u>CF,FK</u>	N		11	D	<u>CF,cF</u>	Food	
3	W	<u>C' K,</u> <u>m</u>	Abs		12	W	<u>M,KF</u> <u>mF</u>	(A), Smoke	
4	D	<u>M,Fc</u> <u>Fm</u>	(H)		13	D	<u>FK,mF,K</u>	Obj	
5	D	<u>Fc,FC'</u>	A	P	14	D	<u>CF,FK</u>	N	
6	W,S	<u>FK,CF</u>	Arch, Bl	O	15	D	<u>CF</u>	N	
7	D	<u>FM,Fc</u>	A		16	D	<u>CF,mF</u>	Blood	
8	W	<u>KF,mF</u>	Clouds		17	W	<u>C'F,cF</u>	N	
9	dr	<u>KF,mF</u>	N		18	W	<u>FM,Fc</u>	A	

Item No.	Loc.	Det.	Con.	P-O	Item No.	Loc.	Det.	Con.	P-O
19	W̊	M,FC'	H	P	40	W	Fm,KF	(Hd), Smoke	
20	D	FM,FC' / Fc	A	O	41	W	C'F,KF / mF	Clouds	
21	W̊	M,FC' / Fc	H		42	W,S	F,C'F	A	P
22	W	KF,C'F	Clouds		43	dr	KF,C'F	Clouds	
23	D	CF,KF	N		44	D	M,Fc	H	O
24	D	FK,CF	Arch, Pl		45	D	FM,CF	A	P
25	D	CF,cF	Obj		46	W	M,Fc	H	
26	D	F,FC	A	+O	47	D	F,K	Obj	
27	D	M,FC / Fc	H	+O	48	W	FK,KF / mF	Explosion	
28	D	FC,Fc	Obj		49	D	FC,Fc	Obj	
29	D	FC,FM	A		50	dd	FK,mF	N	
30	D	M,FC	(H)		51	dr	M,FC'	H	O
31	D	F, FC_{sym}	Hd	+O	52	W	FK,KF / C'F	N	
32	W	FM,Fc	A	P	53	D	FM,Fc	A	
33	D	M,Fc	H		54	D	CF,cF	N	O
34	D	FC,Fc	AAt		55	D	KF	Sky-writing	O
35	D	CF,mF	Fire		56	W	CF,FK	N	
36	D	FK,FC'	Arch		57	W	M−,FC−	H	O−
37	W	CF,FK / mF / KF	N		58	W̊,S	FC,CF	A,Pl	
38	D	FC,Fm	Obj		59	W,S	F,C'F	Obj	
39	W	M,Fc / FC'	H		60	D	M, FC_{sym}	(Hd)	

Appendix 2

Sample Records With Keys

Record Number 1   Male—Age 33 years

Card I
10"

1. Colossus astride Rhodes.

1. Legs are outside lighter gray, head that of a half-wit, these might be his arms. There is a feeling of great strength.

2. The whole blot looks like a symbol for demoniacal flight. (Held for a while and turned)

2. In irrational flight—this seems half-witted, too.

3.√Part of a totem pole, sur-mounted by something that looks like a bald eagle.

3. Totem pole looks carved be-cause of the shading. Here are the wings of eagle.

4. If you look down you see a man in flight, sort of a Leo-nardo da Vinci learning how to fly.

                That's all.

4. Man is in middle and other parts are the wings which be-long to the man—gives you feeling of power, as if Man can fly.

Card II
8"

1. There are two bulls.
2. This might be a butterfly.

2. Shape, it has no head, part of tail, more nearly a moth with open wings, color has nothing to do with it. I never saw a brilliant red butterfly.

3.√Moose's head.

3. —there's the eyes.

4.√Like a spinning top.
5.< Looks like bear's heads—except that the ears are thrown back too far—like young bears.

4. The shape, not in motion.

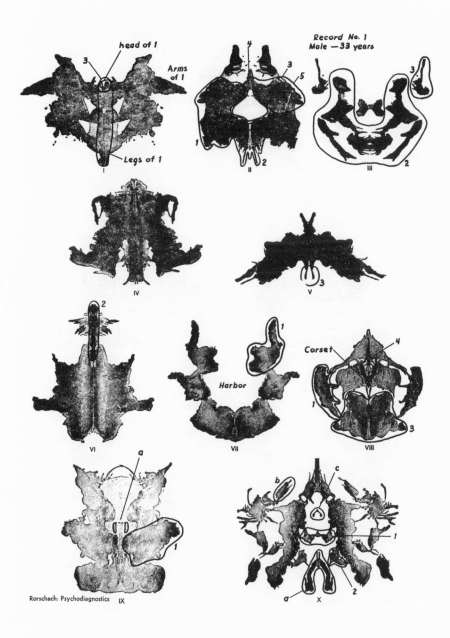

head of 1

3

Arms of 1

Legs of 1

I

Record No. 1
Male — 33 years

II

III

IV

V

VI

Harbor

VII

Corset

VIII

a

Rorschach: Psychodiagnostics   IX

b   c

a   X

Card II (cont.)

Red going through here—just colors—gives a feeling of brownishness which is perfectly consistent with the color of bulls.

Card III

10"

1. Looks like two waiters bowing to one another—either that or they are trying to carry something.

2.√Two Negro boys kicking their feet away—very ludicrous—nothing to do with reality.

3.>See symmetrical spots of blood.

1. They have one leg and one is obscured. It is a caricature, ludicrous.

2. The way their heads look.

3. Color and shading here is important.

   (Q) Just some red symmetrically arranged, doesn't look like anything.

Card IV

25"

I'll be damned!

1. This is a bear skin rug.

   Still looks like bear skin except this (D1) doesn't belong there.

1. Badly dried and cut (Q) because of the dark and light spots in here.

Card V

5"

1. Overelongated moth.

2. Might be representation of a woman decidedly knockkneed, ridiculous headdress, maybe practicing for beaux-art ball.

3.>Beak of a bird.

1. Head—shape of wings cut wrong [extensions not included].

2. More like a silhouette. Never see a man dressed like that; like a Ziegfeld's Folly girl.

Card VI

15"

1. That's a bear skin rug with a piece attached to it that has nothing to do with it

2. Penis there.

1. General shape of skin and shading—skin over back shaded differently—topside—skin out.

Card VII

7"

1. There are two girls made up to look like bunnies—if you take heads alone.

2.√Well protected harbor but it's entirely too symmetrical for a harbor, peculiar contour; must be a coral island, not volcanic.

1. Type of shading reminiscent of Will Cotton's drawings.

2. Harbor unusual but possibly like a topographical map, dark is the land.

Card VIII

2"

1. There are two bears supporting a corset or pulling it apart.

2. Beginning of armorial or escutcheon plate.

3. Looks like a butterfly except colors are wrong. I don't know of any butterflies that go from brown to old rose—butterfly has no head.

4. Vertebra column like an X-ray picture.

1. Four legs, no tail, vestigial on one and not existent on the other.

2. Lots of color design in here.

3. (Q) This butterfly has these colors.

4. The shaded part here.

Card IX

5"

1. There are two William Cotton heads, his color as in the green.

1. Tinge of yellow, greenish blue tinge, there's nose and eye and shock of hair.

(S. tried to do something with orange but couldn't.)

Card **IX** (cont.)

                    a. Eyes of an owl but it is no owl but probably a Cheshire cat.

Card **X**

10"

1. Cross-section of a cervix.

2. Looks like egg yolks dropped down.

                    a. Bunny with peculiar side whiskers, two ears; heavy eyes, shape of head.

                    b. These are bulls with golden horn, it is symbolic, in flight.

                    c. Pawnbroker's golden balls.

Performance Time: 28 minutes.

Note: Total time for each card was not available.

APPENDIX 2

SCORING SHEET

for

Record Number 1

Card No. and Number of Response	Time and Position	Location		Determi- nant		Content		P-O	
		Main	Add	Main	Add	Main	Add	Main	Add

Psychograph
for
Record No. 1

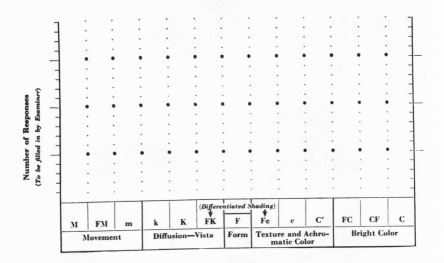

M	FM	m	k	K	FK	F	Fc	c	C'	FC	CF	C
Movement			Diffusion—Vista			Form	Texture and Achromatic Color			Bright Color		

Above the FK and Fc columns: *(Differentiated Shading)*

Left axis label: Number of Responses (To be filled in by Examiner)

Total Responses (R) =

Total Time (T) =

Average time per response $\frac{T}{R}$ =

Average reaction time for
  Cards I, IV, V, VI, VII =

Average reaction time for Cards
  Cards II, III, VIII, IX, X =

$\frac{\text{Total F}}{R}$ =   F%

$\frac{FK + F + Fc}{R}$ =   %

$\frac{A + Ad}{R}$ =   A%

Number of P =

Number of O =

(H + A):(Hd + Ad) =   :

sum C = $\frac{FC + 2CF + 3C}{2}$ =

M: sum C =   :

(FM + m):(Fc + c + C') =   :

$\frac{\text{No. of responses to Cards VIII, IX, X}}{R}$ = %

W:M =   :

Succession:

Rigid   Orderly   Loose   Confused

W   D   d   Dd $\overset{\text{and}}{\underset{\text{or}}{}}$ S

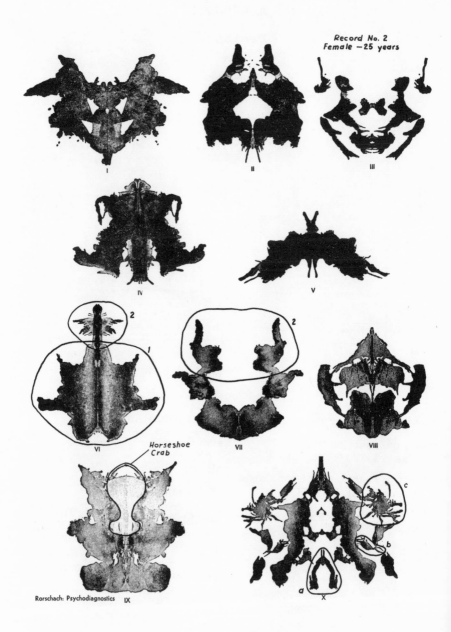

Horseshoe
Crab

Rorschach: Psychodiagnostics   IX

Record Number 2   <u>Female—Age 25 years</u>

<u>Card I</u>

2"

1. Looks like fantastic gar-   1. So many different areas marked
   goyles on a 15th century   out by differences in the card,
   building. Truncated eagle-   could pick out many creatures;
   like creature holding a   two with gesticulating hands;
   crab-like one; like on a   birds-crest with body and claw;
   coat of arms.   just separate masses and fig-
                                       ures; fantastic creatures; one
                                       looks like a bird with animal
                                       hind quarters.

2. A pussycat, the whole thing.   2. Eyes, nose, ears; fantastic cat;
                                       symbolic-representational not
20"   realistically drawn.

<u>Card II</u>

3"

1. Two stout Turks doing a   1. Body, arms, hands, red boots
   ritual dance.   and red turbans, eyes. Women
                                       might wear such turbans but it
                                       made me think more of Turks
10"   because of the fancy clothing;
                                       (Q) heavy draped clothing.

<u>Card III</u>

3"

1. Two surprised and embar-   1. Seat. Men dressed up in eve-
   rassed young men, both have   ning dress, face, noses, eyes;
   discovered that they have   swerving back; the bandstand
   tickets for the same seat.   below in front and decorations
                                       of the theater on side. They
                                       are almost rearing away from
                                       the central object but their
                                       eyes remain looking at it; half
                                       bowing as though they know
15"   they should be polite but each
                                       wants the seat.

<u>Card IV</u>

13"

1. Bug's face magnified (whole).   1. Mottling of some areas, looks

Card IV (Cont.)

like something magnified as
though of different transparen-
cies under a microscope, eyes,
18"   ears, big open jaws and mandi-
ble coming out.

Card V

1"

   1. A bat.

                               1. Can't see parts in relation to
one another; figured it out in
terms of the contrast; wings,
5"   small body, two antennae.

Card VI

3"

   1. A pelt, caught and split   1. Split down the center; backbone;
      down the center and stretched   mottled like a pelt. Middle and
      to dry.   sides dark, edges light as
                                 though pulled; furry side is up,
                               spotted perhaps a leopard's fur,
                               that isn't very furry is it?

   2. Looks like nervous system.   2. Just the emphasis of the center
25"   line and the emanations.

Card VII

15"

   1. Looks like a dissection; parts 1. A lot of organs vaguely con-
      of intestines.   nected with bits of bone and
                               nerve in the middle.

   2. Two women, fighting, only   2. Two women facing, agitated
      their heads. Before the   attitudes, the lines shooting;
      Turks also looked like women. profiles—thrust chin, promi-
                               nent, glaring.
45"

Card VIII

10"

   1. Looks like two animal fig-   1. Bears going sideways on coat
      ures; bears on symbolic coat   of arms. (Q) Coloring symbolic,
      of arms. That's all.   that's all it could be. The pink
                               coming out of orange, conquered
                               green and grey with paw. Saw
                               it moving but it couldn't move

Card VIII (Cont.)

                                          sideways except on a work of
15"   art.

Card IX

10"

1. Skate fish, or horseshoe   1. Colored masses nothing spe-
    crab being washed away by   cific, horseshoe crab washing
    waves (whole).   about in waves, sea-green
25"   water.

Card X

3"

1. Crustacean's ball.   1. Some sort of ball—gay, colorful,
                                        dancers, all animals: a) green
                                        caterpillars, b) lobsters,
                                        c) crayfish; just numerous
7"   crustaceans—gay.

Performance Time: 5 minutes.

APPENDIX 2

SCORING SHEET

for

Record Number 2

Card No. and Number of Response	Time and Position	Location		Determi-nant		Content		P-O	
		Main	Add	Main	Add	Main	Add	Main	Add

Psychograph

for

Record No. 2

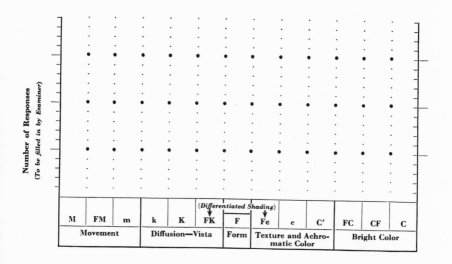

M	FM	m	k	K	FK	F	Fc	c	C'	FC	CF	C
Movement			Diffusion—Vista			Form	Texture and Achromatic Color			Bright Color		

Total Responses (R) =

Total Time (T) =

Average time per response $\dfrac{T}{R} =$

Average reaction time for
  Cards I, IV, V, VI, VII =

Average reaction time for
  Cards II, III, VIII, IX, X =

$\dfrac{\text{Total F}}{R} =$ F%

$\dfrac{FK + F + Fc}{R} =$ %

$\dfrac{A + Ad}{R} =$ A%

Number of P =

Number of O =

(H + A):(Hd + Ad) =

$\text{sum C} = \dfrac{FC + 2CF + 3C}{2} =$

M:sum C =   :

(FM + m):(Fc + c + C') =   :

$\dfrac{\text{No. of responses to Cards VIII,IX,X}}{R} = \%$

W:M =   :

Succession:

Rigid   Orderly   Loose   Confused

W   D   d   Dd $\genfrac{}{}{0pt}{}{\text{and}}{\text{or}}$ S

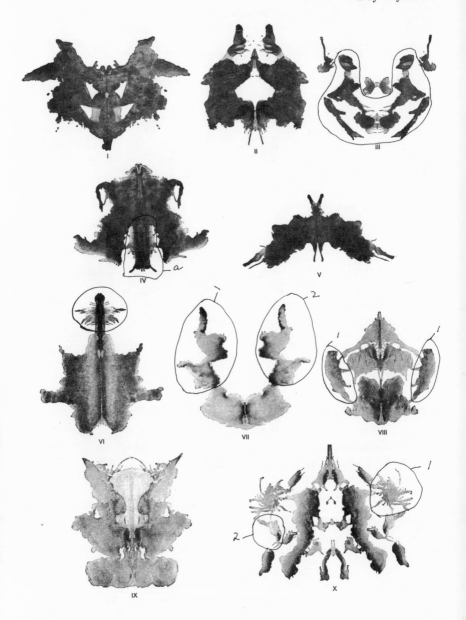

Card I

1"

1. A Chinese person.   1. The eyes, the bumps here, just
                                          the head.

Card II

1"

1. Exploded.   1. Looks like it all exploded, all
                                          of it.

Card III

1"

1. Men.   1. Looks like men here, two of
                                          them.

Card IV

3"

1. A dog.   1. Looks like a dog wearing shoes,
                                          a. with a stand here.

Card V

1"

1. A butterfly.   1. Looks like wings here.

Card VI

3"

1. A airplane.   1. Looks like airplane up here,
                                          wings and body.

Card VII

2"

1.< Two dogs here   1. This way it looks like dogs here,
                                          head and body.

2.∧This could be reindeer here.   2. Looks like reindeer this way, up
                                          here, you know, on the head.

Card VIII

2"

1. Things crawling, could be   1. These look like they're crawling
   ants.   like ants.

Card IX

6"

1. The world.   1. I don't know, just like the
                                         world, like in a book, all the
                                         colors different places.

Card X

2"

1. A lot of different creeper   1. These and these are creeper
   crawlers.   crawlers, all of this.
                                         a. spiders here, and . . .
                                         b. maybe this is a moth,
                                            the spider has lots of legs.

Performance time: 3 minutes

SCORING SHEET

for

Record Number 3

Card No. and Number of Response	Time and Position	Location		Determinant		Content		P-O	
		Main	Add	Main	Add	Main	Add	Main	Add

Psychograph for

Record No. 3

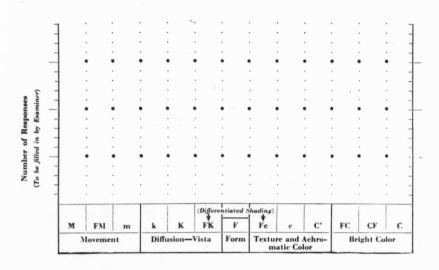

M	FM	m	k	K	FK	F	Fc	c	C'	FC	CF	C
Movement			Diffusion—Vista			Form	Texture and Achromatic Color			Bright Color		

(Differentiated Shading)

Number of Responses *(To be filled in by Examiner)*

Total Responses (R) = Number of P =

Total Time (T) = Number of 0 =

Average time per response $\dfrac{T}{R}$ = (H + A) : (Hd + Ad) = :

Average reaction time for Cards I, IV, V, VI, VII = sum C = $\dfrac{FC + 2CF + 3C}{2}$ =

Average reaction time for Cards II, III, VIII, IX, X = M: sum C = :
(FM + m) : (Fc + c + C') = :

$\dfrac{\text{Total F}}{R}$ = F% $\dfrac{\text{No. of responses to Cards VIII, IX, X}}{R}$ = %

$\dfrac{FK + F + Fc}{R}$ = % W : M = :

$\dfrac{A + Ad}{R}$ = A% Succession

Rigid   Orderly   Loose   Confused

W   D   d   Dd $\dfrac{\text{and}}{\text{or}}$ S

Record Number 4   <u>Boy—Age 8-5 years*</u>

<u>Card I</u>

1"

1. A bird.   1. Here are the wings, the body, and
                                       these could be the antenna.

<u>Card II</u>

7"

1. Two animals, their hands are   1. Here they are, the head, the
   up here.   body, and hands up here.

2. And a butterfly.   2. Right here in the middle.

<u>Card III</u>

3"

1. Oh, two people picking up a   1. People, heads, arms reaching
   bowling ball.   down, look like women because
                                       of the shoes.

<u>Card IV</u>

2"

1. Reminds me of a bat, a design   1. Not exactly a bat, but maybe it
   bat.   could look like a bat, the front
                                       and wings.

<u>Card V</u>

1"

1. A butterfly or a bird.   1. Antenna, wings, a butterfly or a
                                       bird, no really looks more like a
                                       butterfly because of the wings.

<u>Card VI</u>

20"

1. Looks like a painting or a   1. Not really like anything, could be
   design of an animal.   a design of a bird, maybe just
                                       this part like a design of a bird.

<u>Card VII</u>

3"

1. This looks like a design of   1. Dogs here and dogs here, like
   dogs.   this in a design.

Card VIII

4"

1. Two animals going up here.

2. This looks like a skeleton here.

1. Looks like they're crawling up here, some kind of animals.

2. The bones here, maybe the skeleton of a fish.

Card IX

2"

1. A design.

1. This doesn't look like an animal, could be the inside of the body, the colors of different parts like in a book.

Card X

1"

1. Another design of animals.

1. The way it was painted, the shapes.
   a. a moth here
   b. spiders
   c. sea horses and . . .
   d. this looks like two animals with something there, maybe a cigarette.

Performance time: 15 minutes

*A retest of subject presented in Record No. 3.

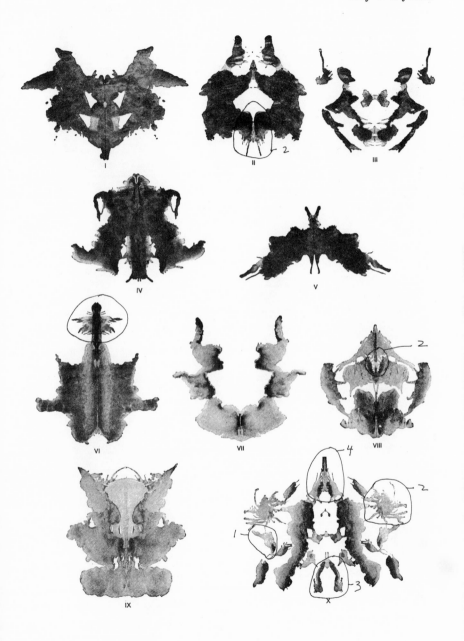

APPENDIX 2

SCORING SHEET

for

Record Number 4

Card No. and Number of Response	Time and Position	Location		Determinant		Content		P-O	
		Main	Add	Main	Add	Main	Add	Main	Add

Psychograph

for

Record No. 4

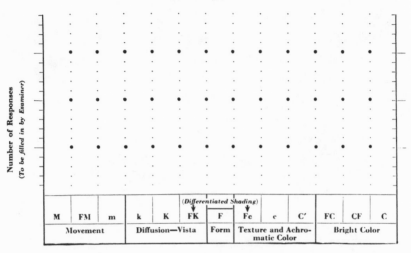

M	FM	m	k	K	FK	F	Fc	c	C'	FC	CF	C
Movement			Diffusion—Vista			Form	Texture and Achromatic Color			Bright Color		

(Differentiated Shading)

Total Responses (R) =

Total Time (T) =

Average time per response $\frac{T}{R}$ =

Average reaction time for
    Cards I, IV, V, VI, VII =

Average reaction time for
    Cards II, III, VIII, IX, X =

$\frac{\text{Total F}}{R}$ =   F%

$\frac{FK + F + Fc}{R}$ =   %

$\frac{A + Ad}{R}$ =   A%

W   D   d   Dd   and
                        or   S

Number of P =

Number of O =

(H + A):(Hd + Ad) =   :

sum C = $\frac{FC + 2CF + 3C}{2}$ =

M: sum C =   :

(FM + m):(Fc + c + C') =   :

$\frac{\text{No. of responses to Cards VIII, IX, X}}{R}$ = %

W:M =   :

Succession:

Rigid   Orderly   Loose   Confused

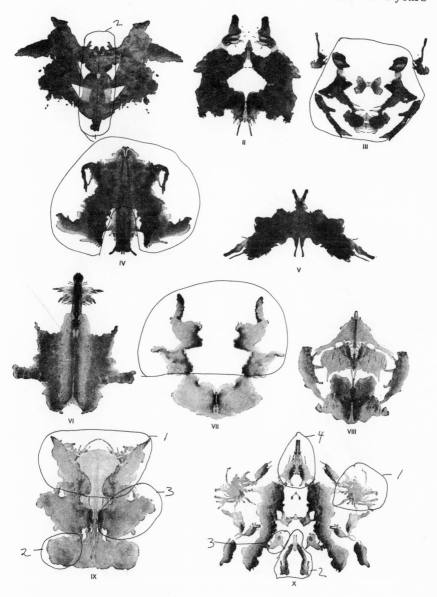

Record Number 5   Girl—Age 13-2 years

Card I

1"

1. A dirty wet street.   1. The blackness, dirty wet street,
                                   like after snow, the blackness
                                   and the different shades.

2. A woman in the middle, her   2. A woman in the middle, you can
   hands up.   see her here, a small waist, the
                                   hands raised up here.

Card II

5"

1. This looks like two people   1. Maybe they are in costume, hats
   dancing.   on their heads, hands up here.

Card III

4"

1. This looks like two people   1. Maybe native women standing over
   standing by a big pot.   a pot.

Card IV

5"

1. Maybe this could be a man   1. It looks funny, he has big feet, his
   with a small head and big   arms are sticking out. I don't know
   feet.   what this could be, it is not part of
                                   the man. The arms are just in that
                                   position.

Card V

1"

1. This just looks like a bat. 1. Wings, body and antenna, just
                                   looks like a bat.

Card VI

4"

1. This could be some sort of   1. Like an area rug, all different
   rug.   things on it, maybe a bear rug,
                                   it doesn't look very flat.

2. This way it could be a cat, a 2. Sort of like a cat, whiskers, the
   cat with a fat body.   body looks fat. legs out here, a
                                   howling sort of cat, like getting
                                   ready to fight.

Card VII

2"

1. Two things looking at each
   other.

    1. Maybe two people waiting to kiss
   each other. Could be two women
   with hair done up like in pictures
   of Greek myths. Just the head and
   shoulders, like you see in the
   pictures.

Card VIII

8"

1. Two animals, maybe lizards
   walking up the sides.

    1. Looks like animals walking up
   something sloping, the angles of
   the legs. Don't know what the
   rest of it is.

Card IX

4"

1. The top looks like two
   lobsters.

    1. The claws and the color looks like
   lobsters.

2. The pink face at the bottom.

    2. Maybe it's someone who is angry
   and his face is red.

3. And all this could be a forest.

    3. The green makes me think of
   leaves in a forest.

Card X

2"

1. Oh this is all kinds of animals—these are spiders.

    1. Here—see lots of legs.

2. Sea horses.

    2. Here sea horses are sometimes
   this color.

3. And here are two cocker
   spaniels, sitting with their
   heads up.

    3. They look so cute, their heads
   are up, spaniels are this color.

4. And these could be parakeets
   biting on something.

    4. These two here, they look like
   they are biting on something here.

Performance time: 30 minutes

APPENDIX 2

SCORING SHEET

for

Record Number 5

Card No. and Number of Response	Time and Position	Location		Deter- minant		Content		P-O	
		Main	Add	Main	Add	Main	Add	Main	Add

Psychograph

for

Record No. 5

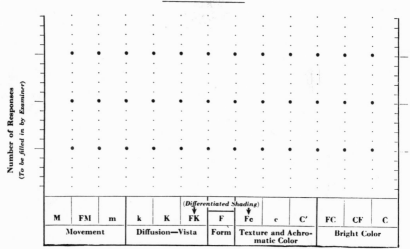

	M	FM	m	k	K	FK	F	Fe	c	C'	FC	CF	C
	Movement			Diffusion—Vista			Form	Texture and Achromatic Color			Bright Color		

(Differentiated Shading)

Total Responses (R) =   Number of P =

Total Time (T) =   Number of O =

Average time per response $\dfrac{T}{R}$ =   (H + A):(Hd + Ad) =   :

Average reaction time for   sum C = $\dfrac{FC + 2CF + 3C}{2}$ =
 Cards I, IV, V, VI, VII =

                                                 M: sum C =   :
Average reaction time for
 Cards II, III, VIII, IX, X =   (FM + m):(Fc + c + C') =   :

$\dfrac{\text{Total F}}{R}$ =   F% $\dfrac{\text{No. of responses to Cards VIII, IX, X}}{R}$ =%

$\dfrac{FK + F + Fc}{R}$ =   %   W:M =   :

$\dfrac{A + Ad}{R}$ =   A%   Succession:

W   D   d   Dd $\genfrac{}{}{0pt}{}{\text{and}}{\text{or}}$ S   Rigid   Orderly   Loose   Confused

KEY

Record No. 1

Male—Age 33 years

Card No. and Number of Response	Time and Position	Location		Determinant		Content		P-O	
		Main	Add	Main	Add	Main	Add	Main	Add
I	10"								
1.		W		M		(H)		O	
2.		W		mF		Abs		O	
3.	∨	dr		Fc		Obj	A	O	
4.	>	W		M		(H)		O	
II	8"								
1.		D		F	FC	A		P	O
2.		D		F		A			
3.	∨	D		F		Ad			
4.	∨	S		F		Obj			
5.	< ⋜ ∨	D		F		Ad			
III	10"								
1.		Ẅ		M		H		P	
2.	∨	Ẅ		M		H			
3.	>	D		CF	cF	Blood			
IV	25"								
1.		Ẅ		Fc		Aobj			
V	5"								
1.		Ẅ		F		A		P	
2.		W		M		H			
3.	>	d		F		Ad			

APPENDIX 2

KEY (Con't.)

Record No. 1
Male—Age 33 years

Card No. and Number of Response	Time and Position	Location		Determinant		Content		P-O	
		Main	Add	Main	Add	Main	Add	Main	Add
VI	15 "								
1.		W		Fc		Aobj		P	
2.		D		F		Sex			
VII	7 "								
1.		D		Fc		Hd	Art		
2.	∨	S	W	Fk		Geo			
VIII	2 "								
1.		D		FM	F	A	Obj	P	O
2.		W		CF		Obj			
3.		D		FC		A			
4.		D		Fk		At			
IX	5 "								
1.		D		FC		Hd	Art		
a.			S		F		Ad		
X	10 "								
1.		D		F		Sex			
2.		D		CF		Food			
a.			D		F		Ad	P	
b.			D		FM FC		A		O
c.			D		FC		Obj		

KEY (Con't.)—Record No. 1
The Psychograph

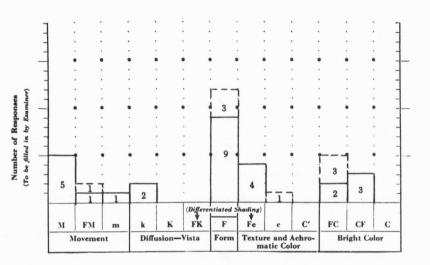

Total Responses (R) = 27 + 4

Total Time (T) = 28'

Average time per response $\frac{T}{R}$ =1'

Average reaction time for Cards
I, IV, V, VI, VII = 12"

Average reaction time for Cards
II, III, VIII, IX, X = 7"

$\frac{\text{Total F}}{R}$ = 33 F%

$\frac{FK + F + Fc}{R}$ = 48%

$\frac{A + Ad}{R}$ = 30 A%

W% = 37; D% = 48; d% = 4;
   Dd + S% = 11

Number of P = 5 + 1

Number of O = 3 + 4

(H + A):(Hd + Ad) = 10:5

sum C = $\frac{FC + 2CF + 3C}{2}$ = 4

M:sum C = 5:4

(FM + m):(Fc + c + C') = 2:4

$\frac{\text{No. of responses to Cards VIII,IX,X}}{R}$=26%

W:M = 10:5

Succession:

Rigid   Orderly   Loose   Confused

APPENDIX 2

KEY

Record No. 2
Female—Age 25 years

Card No. and Number of Response	Time and Position	Location		Determinant		Content		P-O	
		Main	Add	Main	Add	Main	Add	Main	Add
I	2"								
1.		W		FM	Fc	(A)	Arch		O
2.		W	S	F		Ad			
II	3"								
1.		W		M	FC, Fc	H			
III	3"								
1.		W		M		H		P	
IV	13"								
1.		W		Fc		Ad			
V	1"								
1.		W		F		A		P	
VI	3"								
1.		D		Fc		Aobj		P	
2.		D		F		At			
VII	15'								
1.		W		F		At			
2.		D		M		Hd			
VIII	10"								
1.		W		FM	Csym	A	Art	P	O
IX	10"								
1.		W		F	CF, mF	A	N		
X	3"								
1.		W		CF sym	M	(A)			
a)		D			FC		A		P
b)		D			F		A		
c)		D			F		A		P

KEY (Con't.)—Record No. 2

The Psychograph

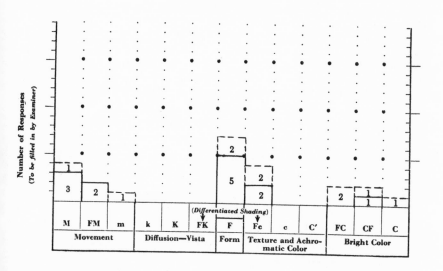

RELATIONSHIPS AMONG FACTORS

Total Responses (R) = 13 + 3

Total Time (T) = 5 min

Average time per response $\frac{T}{R}$ = 23 "

Average reaction time for Cards
I, IV, V, VI, VII = 10"

Average reaction time for Cards
II, III, VIII, IX, X = 6"

$\frac{\text{Total F}}{R}$ = 38 F%

$\frac{FK + F + Fc}{R}$ = 54%

$\frac{A + Ad}{R}$ = 54 A%

Manner of Approach

W(77%); D(23%); d(0%); D d $_{\text{or}}^{\text{and}}$ S(0%)

Number of P = 4 + 2

Number of O = 0 + 2

(H + A):(Hd + Ad) = 8:2

sum C = $\frac{FC + 2CF + 3C}{2}$ = 1

M:sum C = 3:1

(FM + m):(Fc + c + C') = 2:2

$\frac{\text{No. of responses to Cards VIII, IX, X}}{R}$ = 23%

W:M = 10:3

Succession:

Rigid	Orderly	Loose	Confused

APPENDIX 2

KEY

Record No. 3

Boy–Age 5 years

Card No. and Number of Response	Time and Position	Location		Determinant		Content		P-O	
		Main	Add	Main	Add	Main	Add	Main	Add
I	1"								
1.		W	S	F		Hd			
II	1"								
1.		W		m		exp			
III	1"								
1.		W		F		H			
IV	3"								
1.		W		F–		A			
a.			D		F		obj		
V	1"								
1.		W		F		A		P	
VI	3"								
1.		D		F–		obj			
VII	2"								
1.	<	D		F		A			
2.	∧	D		F		Ad			
VIII	2"								
1.		D		FM		A			
IX	6"								
1.		W		C/F		world			
X	2"								
1.		W		F		A			
a.			D		F		A		P
b.			D		F		A		

KEY (Cont.)–Record No. 3

The Psychograph

Total Responses (R) = 11   Number of P = 1

Total Time (T) = 3'   Number of O = 0

Average time per response $\frac{T}{R}$ = 16"   (H + A):(Hd + Ad) = 6:2

Average reaction time for
  Cards I, IV, V, VI, VII = 2"   sum C = $\frac{FC + 2CF + 3C}{2}$ = 0

                                                     M: sum C = 0:1

Average reaction time for
  Cards II, III, VIII, IX, X = 2"   (FM + m):(FC + c + C') = 2:0

$\frac{\text{Total F}}{R}$ =   73 F% $\frac{\text{No. of responses to Cards VIII, IX, X}}{R}$ = 27%

$\frac{FK + F + Fc}{R}$ =   73%   W:M = 7:0

$\frac{A + Ad}{R}$ =   55 A%   Succession:

W% = 64; D% = 36; d% = 0;

Dd $\begin{smallmatrix} \text{and} \\ \text{or} \end{smallmatrix}$ S% = 0

| Rigid | Orderly | Loose | Confused |

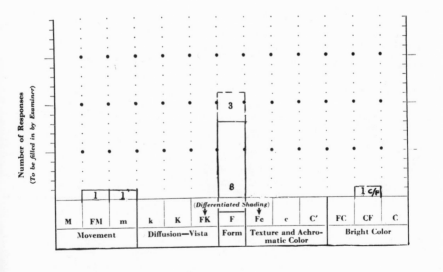

APPENDIX 2

KEY

Record No. 4

Boy—Age 8-5 years

Card No. and Number of Response	Time and Position	Location Main	Location Add	Determinant Main	Determinant Add	Content Main	Content Add	P-O Main	P-O Add
I	1"								
1.		W		F		A		P	
II	7"								
1.		W		F →	FM	A			
2.		D		F		A			
III	3"								
1.		W̶		M		H		P	
IV	2"								
1.		W		F−		A			
V	1"								
1.		W		F		A		P	
VI	20"								
1.		D		F		(A)			
VII	3"								
1.		W		F		(A)			
VIII	4"								
1.		D →	W	FM		A		P	
2.		D		F		At			
IX	2"								
1.		W		C/F		At			
X	1"								
1.		W		F		(A)			
a.			D		F		A		
b.			D		F		A		P
c.			D		F		A		
d.			D		F		A		

KEY (Cont.)–Record No. 4

The Psychograph

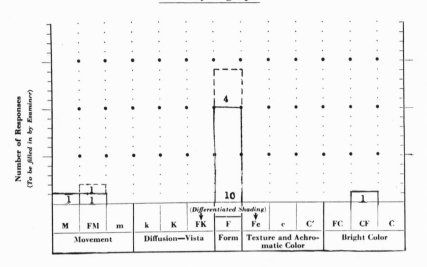

1	1					10					1	
					(Differentiated Shading) ↓							
M	**FM**	**m**	**k**	**K**	**FK**	**F**	**Fc**	**c**	**C'**	**FC**	**CF**	**C**
Movement			Diffusion—Vista			Form	Texture and Achro-matic Color			Bright Color		

Total Responses (R) = 12

Total Time (T) = 15'

Average time per response $\frac{T}{R}$ = 75"

Average reaction time for Cards I, IV, V, VI, VII = 5"

Average reaction time for Cards II, III, VIII, IX, X = 3"

$\frac{\text{Total F}}{R}$ =   75 F%

$\frac{FK + F + Fc}{R}$ =   75%

$\frac{A + Ad}{R}$ =   75 A%

W% = 67; D% = 33; d% = 0;

Dd $^{\text{and}}_{\text{or}}$ S% = 0

Number of P = 4

Number of O = 0

(H + A):(Hd + Ad) = 10:0

sum C = $\frac{FC + 2CF + 3C}{2}$ = 1

M: sum C = 1:1

(FM + m):(FC + c + C') = 1:0

$\frac{\text{No. of responses to Cards VIII, IX, X}}{R}$ = 33%

W:M   8:1

Succession:

Rigid	Orderly	Loose	Confused

APPENDIX 2

KEY

Record No. 5

Girl–Age 13-2 years

Card No. and Number of Response	Time and Position	Location		Determinant		Content		P-O	
		Main	Add	Main	Add	Main	Add	Main	Add
I	1"								
1.		W		C'F	cF	obj			
2.		D		M		H			
II	5"								
1.		W		M		H			
III	4"								
1.		W̶		M		H		P	
IV	5"								
1.		W̶		F		H			
V	1"								
1.		W		F		A		P	
VI	4"								
1.		W		Fc		Aobj		P	
2.	V	W		FM		A			
VII	2"								
1.		W̶		M		(Hd)			
VIII	8"								
1.		D →	W	FM		A		P	
IX	4"								
1.		D		FC		A			
2.		D		FC	Fm	Hd			
3.		D		CF		Plant			

KEY (Cont.)

Record No. 5

Girl—Age 13-2 years

Card No. and Number of Response	Time and Position	Location		Determinant		Content		P-O	
		Main	Add	Main	Add	Main	Add	Main	Add
X	2"								
1.		D		F		A		P	
2.		D		FC		A			
3.		D		FM	FC	A			
4.		D		FM		A			

KEY (Cont.)—Record No. 5

The Psychograph

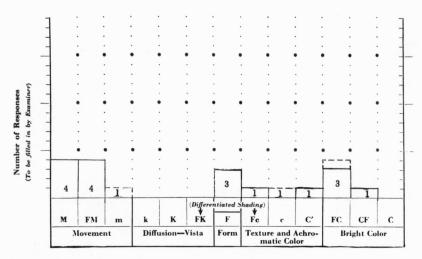

M	FM	m	k	K	FK	F	Fc	c	C'	FC	CF	C
4	4	1̄				3	1̄	1̄	1	3	1̄	
Movement			Diffusion—Vista			Form	Texture and Achromatic Color			Bright Color		

(Differentiated Shading)

Total Responses (R) = 17

Total Time (T) = 30'

Average time per response $\frac{T}{R}$ = 2'

Average reaction time for Cards I, IV, V, VI, VII = 3."

Average reaction time for Cards II, III, VIII, IX, X = 5"

$\frac{\text{Total F}}{R}$ = 18 F%

$\frac{FK + F + Fc}{R}$ = 24%

$\frac{A + Ad}{R}$ = 47 A%

W% = 47; D% = 53; d% = 0;

Dd $\overset{\text{and}}{\underset{\text{or}}{}}$ S% = 0

Number of P = 5

Number of O = 0

(H + A):(Hd + Ad) = 12:2

sum C = $\frac{FC + 2CF + 3C}{2}$ = 2.5

M: sum C = 4:2.5

(FM + m):(FC + c + C') = 4:2

$\frac{\text{No. of responses to Cards VIII, IX, X}}{R}$ = 47%

W:M = 8:4

Succession:

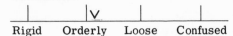

| Rigid | Orderly | Loose | Confused |

Appendix 3

Comparative Table of Location and Determinant Scores[1]

		This Manual	Rorschach (1951)	Beck (1967)	Piotrowski (1957)	Rapaport et al. (1968)
Location Scores		W	W	W	W	W
		W̄				
		DW	DW	DW	DW	DW
		D	D	D	D	D
		d	D	Dd	d	Dd
		Dd (dd,de,di,dr)	Dd	Dd	d	Dr,De,Do
		S	S	Ds,Dds	S	S (large area) s (small area)
Form Scores		F+	F+	F+	F+	F+
		F	F+	F,F+,F−	F±	F+ or F∓
		F−	F−	F−	F−	F−
Movement Scores		M	M	M	M	M
		FM			FM	FM[2]
		Fm,mF,m		M (sometimes)	m (inanimate movement)	
Chromatic Color Scores		FC	FC	FC	FC	FC
		F/C				F/C
		CF	CF	CF	CF	CF
		C/F				C/F
		C	C	C	C	C
		Cn			Cn	C
		Cdes			Cn	C
		Csym				C
Achromatic Color Scores		FC',C'F,C'		FY,YF,Y (when black or gray)	Fc',c' (if dysphoric) FCw,CwF,Cw (if white)[4]	FC',C'F,C'
SHADING SCORES	Texture & Surface	Fc,cF,c	F(C)[3]	FT,TF,T	Fc,c[4]	FCh,ChF,Ch F(C) shading used to outline an object
	Diffusion Vista	FK	F(C)[3]	FV,VF,V (according to emphasis on V)	Fc[4]	
		KF,K	F(C)[3]	Y (for diffuse black, for all white, for abstraction)	c'[4]	ChF,Ch
	Depth	Fk,kF,k	F(C)[3]	FY,YF,Y	c[4] c' if dysphoric	ChF,Ch

[1] For more detailed explanation of all scores, see references.
[2] Used to denote weak human action or animals in human-like motion. Animals in motion are usually not scored M or FM.
[3] Rorschach used this symbol for all qualities of light and shadow.
[4] Used by Piotrowski to denote specific qualities.

References

Allen, R. M. (1953), Introduction to the Rorschach Technique: a Manual of Administration and Scoring. New York: International Universities Press.

Ames, L. B. et al. (1974), Child Rorschach Responses; Developmental Trends from Two to Ten Years. New York: Brunner/Mazel.

Ames, L. B., Metraux, R. W. & Walker, R. N. (1971), Adolescent Rorschach Responses; Developmental Trends from Ten to Sixteen Years. (Rev. Ed.) New York: Brunner/Mazel.

Beck, S. J. (1967), Rorschach's Test. I–Basic Processes. (3rd Ed.) New York: Grune & Stratton.

Hertz, M. R. (1960), The Rorschach in Adolescence. In: Projective Techniques with Children, ed. A. I. Rabin & M. R. Haworth. New York: Grune & Stratton.

Klopfer, B. et al. (1954), Developments in the Rorschach Technique, Vol. I. Technique and Theory. New York: Harcourt Brace Jovanovich.

Klopfer, B. & Davidson, H. H. (1962), The Rorschach Technique: An Introductory Manual. New York: Harcourt Brace Jovanovich.

Levitt, E. E. & Truumaa, A. (1972), The Rorschach Technique with Children and Adolescents. New York: Grune & Stratton.

Ledwith, N. H. (1960), A Rorschach Study of Child Development. Pittsburgh: Pa. University of Pittsburgh Press.

Piotrowski, Z. A. (1957), Perceptanalysis. New York: Macmillan.

Rabin, A. I. & Haworth, M. R. (1960), Projective Techniques with Children. New York: Grune & Stratton.

Rapaport, D., Gill, M. M. & Schafer, R. (1968), Diagnostic Psychological Testing (Rev. Ed.). New York: International Universities Press.

Rorschach, H. (1951), Psychodiagnostics. (5th Ed.) Berne, Switzerland: Verlag Hans Huber.

Small, L. (1956), Rorschach Location and Scoring Manual. New York: Grune & Stratton.